YO-BRA-522

PERSONAL SAFETY AND DEFENSE FOR WOMEN

by

F. PATRICIA PECHANEC STOCK, M. S.

Physical Activities Department
University of California
Santa Barbara
Santa Barbara, California

Illustrations by
KATHARINE M. BARTHELS, M.A.

Burgess Publishing Company
426 South Sixth Street • Minneapolis, Minn. 55415

Consulting Editor to the Publisher

Eloise M. Jaeger, Ph.D.
    Head, Department of Physical Education for Women
    University of Minnesota
    Minneapolis

To my husband, Vincent Eugene Stock

PREFACE

In the United States each year law enforcement agencies report an increase in criminal behavior. These annual increases indicate society's failure to eliminate crime and law enforcement's inability to control crime. As a result, the individual faces the increased possibility of becoming the victim of a criminal. According to the 1966 F.B.I. Crime Clock Chart, there is one murder every forty-eight minutes; one forcible rape every twenty-one minutes; one aggravated assault every two minutes; one robbery every three and one-half minutes; one burglary every twenty-three seconds; one larceny ($50 and over) every thirty-six seconds; and one auto theft every fifty-seven seconds. To avoid becoming the victim of a criminal, each person must assume greater responsibility for the safety and protection of his property and person.

This book is designed to help all women learn how to avoid becoming the victim of a criminal. Part One, a discussion of the nature and causes of crime, difficulties in reporting crime, and problems of deterring crime, demonstrates the need for learning personal defense. Parts Two and Three list devices to use and precautions to take for property protection and personal safety and for effectively deterring and avoiding criminals. Part Four presents the weapon skills and personal defense techniques of counterattack to employ in order to escape the direct physical attack of a criminal. One hundred and fifty-five illustrations show how to execute the skills and techniques of self-defense. *Personal Safety and Defense for Women* is a book to read and a program to learn, practice, perfect, and use continuously.

ACKNOWLEDGEMENTS

I am greatly indebted to many persons for their help in the preparation of this work. I am especially grateful to my husband, Vincent E. Stock, for his suggestions and encouragement.

Special thanks are extended to the defense technique models, Richard Barthels and Katharine Barthels.

I also wish to thank Brigitte Koehler who did the rapidograph and zip-a-tone of all the illustrations drawn by Katharine M. Barthels.

I am grateful to all my students at the University of California Santa Barbara and to my University of California Extension Division students who have given me insight, information and encouragement to write this text. This is the kind of book my students feel will serve all women who are interested in protecting their lives and property.

TABLE OF CONTENTS

PART I

THE NEED FOR PERSONAL DEFENSE

Chapter One

CRIME
AS IT CONCERNS
PERSONAL DEFENSE

INTRODUCTION

Increased urbanization with its attendant economic, social and psychological frictions has been matched by significant increases in crime, which neither the city governments nor the federal government have been able to curb. Mid-century America is undergoing a serious social upheaval. It is a time of bewildering contradictions: prosperity versus poverty, black versus white, haves versus have-nots, the old ethic of work versus the new reality of leisure. The basis of our society, the family, seems threatened. Respect for authority, once self-imposed through training or imposed by legal authorities, has diminished in the wake of the tensions caused by current living conditions. As might be expected, crime deterrence has not been able to keep pace with crime. Therefore, the individual must assume more responsibility for defense of his person and property. A knowledge of crime, its characteristics, and its frequency can help a person — and you — avoid becoming a victim.

CRIME CLASSIFICATIONS

Crimes are categorized according to the penalties ascribed to the acts committed or according to the nature of the acts themselves. Throughout the United States crimes are classified as either felonies or misdemeanors. Felonies are crimes punishable by death or by more than one year imprisonment; all other crimes are misdemeanors. However, each state has its own penal code according to which it fixes penalties; therefore, an act that is a felony in one state may be a misdemeanor in another, or not a crime at all in a third state.

Crimes that most states consider felonies are burglary, auto theft, larceny, criminal homicide, robbery, aggravated assault, forcible rape, and the violation of laws pertaining to the use of drugs. All other crimes are misdemeanors, which account for eight-five percent of all arrests.[1]

In terms of personal defense crimes are defined according to the nature of the acts themselves, either violations against property or violations against the person. Property crimes generally occur during the victim's absence, while personal crimes are committed directly against the victim's body. Techniques of safety and personal defense presented in Parts II, III, and IV are based on this distinction.

---

[1]"Meaningless Statistics", *Time Magazine,* LXXXVIII (August 19, 1966), p. 48.

CRIMES AGAINST PROPERTY

Burglary, auto theft, and larceny are crimes against property which may result in the loss of your possessions. The definitions for these property crimes are based on the F.B.I.'s *Uniform Crime Reports in the United States*[2] and on the "Standard Offense Classification for Criminal Statistics,"[3] which has been adopted by the Judicial Section of the American Bar Association and the National Conference of Judicial Councils:

> Burglary. All offenses in which any building or structure is broken into or entered with the intention of committing a felony, or any theft therein any time of day or night. Also includes any unlawful entry to commit a felony or theft, even when no force is used to gain entry.

> Auto Theft. All offenses in which a motor vehicle is stolen, or driven away and abandoned by someone not having lawful access to the vehicle.

> Larceny. Theft of articles valued $50 and over. Includes thefts of bicycles, automobile accessories, shop lifting, pocket-picking, or any stealing of property or article of value which is not taken by force, violence, or fraud.

Frequency of Property Crimes

During each minute of 1966 one larceny, one auto theft, and two burglaries were committed in the United States.[4] *Uniform Crime Reports* data presented in Chart I show that property crime arrests totaled 2,821,900 in 1966. Of this total burglaries accounted for almost half. Property crimes occurred equally throughout the country. Over a ten year period the peak month for burglary and larceny has been December.

Chart I. FREQUENCY OF PROPERTY CRIMES ACCORDING TO REGIONS AND PEAK MONTHS.

Ten Year Trend of Peak Months	Crimes Against Property	1966 Total Reported Cases In U.S.	Percentage Occurring In:			
			Southern States	North Central States	North-eastern States	Western States
December	BURGLARY	1,370,300	28%	23%	24%	25%
October	AUTO THEFT	557,000	23%	27%	28%	22%
August & December	LARCENY	894,600	26%	23%	26%	25%

Figures taken from *Uniform Crime Reports in the United States, 1966,* pp. 15, 18, 22, 25. These figures are based on reported crime received from law enforcement agencies representing 92% of the national population.

Relationship of Drug Addiction and Property Crime

Since much of the crime committed against property involves the narcotic addict, who needs on the average of $10.00-$40.00 per day to support his habit, it becomes increasingly important for the student of personal defense to understand the role of the narcotic addict in crime.

---

[2]J. Edgar Hoover, *Uniform Crime Reports in the United States, 1966* (Washington D.C., U.S. Government Printing Office, 1967), p. 55.

[3]Ronald H. Beattie, *Crime in California 1964* (Sacramento, California, Bureau of Criminal Statistics, 1964), pp. 181-182.

[4]Hoover, *op. cit.,* p. 21.

In order to get enough money to buy drugs, the addict bleeds his family and friends; he lies, cheats, and steals. When these resources are exhausted, the addict resorts to bigger crimes. In and out of police courts, jails and hospitals, he represents a constant drain on the taxpayer's dollars in our country.[5]

The most frequent type of crime committed by the addict is burglary. Television sets, radios, typewriters, adding machines, jewelry, equipment, trucks, and auto accessories are articles sought by the drug addict. These articles are sold to a fence (a dealer in stolen goods) for ten to twenty-five percent of their actual value. The addict often acts out of sheer desperation, and so he can be dangerous. Frequently very little planning occurs prior to a burglary executed by the addict. He ransacks a place using little discrimination as to what he steals. He leaves drawers overturned and generally makes a mess of everything he touches.[6] After the burglary the addict often discovers that he has taken dime store jewelry, broken alarm clocks, and other worthless items which cannot be sold to a fence.

Since the sole motive for an addict committing burglary is money to support his habit, currency is one of the most sought after items. Beach areas have become common sites for him to work because he knows many people leave their wallets or purses in their automobiles before going down to the water for a swim. If the car is left unlocked, the victim inadvertently assist the thief.

In the same way, unfortunately, much property loss through burglary, auto theft, and larceny is partly attributable to the law-abiding citizen who becomes victimized because of his own ignorance or carelessness. For example, at least forty-two percent of all stolen automobiles had keys left in the ignitions, or the ignitions were left unlocked.[7] The obvious defense technique for you to take when leaving a parked car would be always to lock it, taking the keys with you. For a detailed treatment of defense measures to take for safekeeping of property and possessions refer to Part II.

CRIMES AGAINST THE PERSON

The second type of crime for which individuals must learn defense is crime against the person. Crimes which may cause death or bodily injury include criminal homicide, robbery, aggravated assault, and forcible rape. The definitions for these personal crimes are based on the F.B.I's *Uniform Crime Reports in the United States,*[8] and on the "Standard Offense Classification for Criminal Statistics."[9]

Criminal Homicide. All degrees of murder and all types of manslaughter by negligence — including vehicular.

Robbery. All offenses in which property is taken from the person, or in the immediate presence of another, by force, violence or threat. Also includes strong-arm robbery, stick-ups, assault with intent to rob, and any attempt to commit robbery.

Aggravated Assault. Assault with intent to kill or attempted assaults which may result in death or assault for the purpose of inflicting severe bodily injury by stabbing, shooting, maiming,

---

[5]Victor H. Vogel, M.D., *Facts About Drug Addiction* (Chicago, Illinois, Science Research Associates, 1965), p. 10.

[6]Gene Accas and John H. Eckstein, *How To Protect Yourself on the Streets and In Your Home* (New York, Pocket Books, Inc., 1965), pp. 39-41.

[7]"Rising Crime Is An Immediate Problem and Needs Answer Now", *Los Angeles Times* (January 29, 1968), Part II, p. 5, Columns 3-4.

[8]Hoover, *op. cit.,* p. 55.

[9]Beattie, *op. cit.,* pp. 181-182.

poisoning, scalding, or by the use of acids, explosives, or other means. Does not include assault to commit robbery, rape, simple assault, assault and battery, or fighting.

Forcible Rape. Rape is forcible rape when the female is (a). overcome by force and is unable to resist, (b). declared a lunatic, (c). declared mentally incompetent, (d). intoxicated, (e). drugged, (f). afraid of immediate bodily injury or harm, (g). unconscious of the nature of the act, or (h). under the belief that the perpetrator is her husband. Includes attempted rape and assault to rape.

Frequency of Personal Crimes

Personal crimes, unlike property crimes, appear to be unequally distributed throughout the United States according to *Uniform Crime Reports in the United States, 1966.* The Southern states reported a higher percentage of murders, aggravated assaults, and forcible rapes than any other region. The same report indicates that throughout the United States aggravated assaults occurred twenty-three (23) times more frequently than murders, which rank the lowest among crimes against the person.

The season of the year seems to influence the rate of crimes committed, as shown in Chart II. Over a ten year period more robberies were committed in November and December than during any other months of the year, while forcible rapes were committed more frequently from April through September. Part III analyzes precautionary measures to take for personal safety against such crimes.

Chart II. FREQUENCY OF CRIMES AGAINST THE PERSON ACCORDING TO REGIONS AND MONTHS

Ten Year Trend of Peak Months	Crimes Against The Person	1966 Total Reported Cases In U.S.	Percentage Occurring In:			
			Southern States	North Central States	North- eastern States	Western States
December	MURDERS	10,920	49%	22%	16%	13%
November & December	ROBBERY	153,420	22%	34%	26%	18%
July & August	AGGRAVATED ASSAULT	231,800	40%	22%	20%	18%
April through Sept.	FORCIBLE RAPE	25,330	29%	27%	19%	25%

Figures taken from *Uniform Crime Reports in the United States, 1966,* pp. 4-13. These figures are based on reported crime received from law enforcement agencies representing 92% of the national population.

SUMMARY

In Chapter One and throughout the book, only the more serious crimes, felonies, are discussed. Each felony committed has a victim; an owner's property or a person's body. Approximately three and one-quarter million (3,250,000) felony arrests were made in 1966, (Charts I and II). Therefore, three and one-quarter million citizens were victims of the felony crimes against property — burglary, larceny and auto theft —, or were victims of the felony crimes against person — murder, robbery, aggravated assault and forcible rape. The crime problem is not simply a legal or police matter; it is primarily a threat to each citizen, each a potential victim.

Chapter Two

CURRENT PROBLEMS
IN CRIME STUDY

INTRODUCTION

Crime is a social problem which concerns all citizens and all communities. All suffer the consequences of crime directly as victims or indirectly as taxpayers. To help deter crime and to avoid becoming a victim, you must be aware of current trends in crimes committed. In this respect, as you have seen in Chapter One, statistics can be helpful. However, typical difficulties that arise in utilizing crime statistics are their inaccuracy in identifying crimes, in determining who commit them, and in assessing the costs of crime to the taxpayer.

CRIME STATISTICS AND THEIR ACCURACY

Since 1960 the crime rate has increased forty-eight percent, nine times as fast as the population growth. [10] Arrests for Narcotic Drug Law Violations have risen eighty-two percent between 1960-1966 with twenty-eight percent of this rise occurring between 1965 and 1966. [11]

Such crime statistics are familiar to every reader, but they are shocking and meaningless to most. For without additional information — Who collected the data? When? Where? How? — accurate conclusions cannot be drawn. Crime statistics, like all statistics, must be examined with great care; they may be inaccurate in their compilation or interpretation.

Compilation

Until recently criminal statistics have been misleading, vague, and often distorted. Statisticians have a difficult time compiling accurate crime statistics because many law enforcement agencies do not report their total records to any one central agency. Statistics for the F.B.I. are submitted by local law enforcement agencies on a voluntary basis only. Additional difficulties in collecting accurate crime data occur because State Penal Codes frequently disagree in defining and identifying specific crimes. For example, adultery is a crime in only forty-five out of the fifty states; however, it serves as a ground for an absolute divorce in all fifty states. Adultery, a felony in Connecticut, is not a crime at all in Arkansas, California, Louisana, New Mexico, and Tennessee.[12]

One central agency, the F.B.I. collects and annually publishes crime statistics under the title, *Uniform Crime Reports in the United States.* Many lawyers and sociologists question the quality of F.B.I. statistics because their data are compiled from police

---

[10]Hoover, *op. cit.,* p. 2.
[11]*Ibid.,* p. 1.
[12]Samuel G. Kling, *Sexual Behavior And The Law* (New York, Bernard Geis Associates, 1965), pp. 15-16.

departments, many of which report crimes in different ways, or in order to soothe the public do not report crimes. For example, Philadelphia reported a startling seventy percent improvement in crime prevention for a four year period. How was this achieved? One complete police district failed to report. [13] It is also argued that F.B.I. reports are erroneous because they consider only "serious crimes", but do not include in their reporting the "less serious crimes" which constitute eighty-five percent of all arrests. [14] Nevertheless, if we keep in mind the limited accuracy of all crime statistics, the F.B.I. reports can be valuable since they serve as guidelines concerning at least some of the crimes committed in the United States.

Interpretation

In interpreting crime statistics, it is essential to remember that, in all reports and in this book, they are based on reported crime rather than real crime. Real crime, an unknown illegal act, is not considered a crime until reported. Because we have no information about real crime, to say the crime rate has increased 10% is to mean that the reported crime rate has increased 10%.

On the other hand we do have knowledge of a sharp increase and sophistication in the detection and reporting of crime. Therefore, the reported crime rates from one year to another cannot be compared accurately over a period of years. In fact, the boom in crime in the past five years is a boom in reported crime, and it is partially due to superior reporting by more agencies.

Greater cooperation of the various law enforcement agencies is constantly improving the accuracy of crime statistics. There is a growing uniformity in the definition of terms; and computers are improving the collection, centralization and tabulation of crime data. With full cooperation the true scope of crime could be more accurately ascertained. In order to reduce current crime rates in our country, we must have up-to-date, accurate statistics concerning crime facts. Therefore, all agencies involved in the administration of criminal justice should act responsibly in their respective roles of compiling and interpreting reliable statistics. [15] Now let us see what some statistics do reveal about crime.

DETERMINING WHO COMMIT CRIMES

Age Groups

What age groups in our society are responsible for committing crime? Of all criminal arrests in 1966, twenty-one percent were juveniles. [16] Eighteen-year-olds and under participated in thirty-four percent of the nation's crimes, [17] while seventy-five percent of all arrests were of people under twenty-five years of age (see the percentage table below). The fifteen through seventeen year old age group represented 5.4% of the population and accounted for the following share of arrests for serious crimes:

---

[13]*Time Magazine, op. cit.,* p. 48.

[14]*Loc. cit.*

[15]Hoover, *op. cit.,* p. v.

[16]Ronald H. Beattie and John P. Kenney, "Aggressive Crimes", *The Annals of the American Academy of Political and Social Science,* CLXIV (Philadelphia, March 1966), pp. 73-85.

[17]*Arizona Daily Star* (August 9, 1965), Section A, p. 1.

PERCENTAGE TABLE

All arrests	12.9%	
Murder	7.0%	
Aggravated Assault	15.0%	
Forcible rape	14.0%	(under 25 years of age, 64%)
Robbery	30.0%	(under 25 years of age, 69%)
Burglary	51.0%	(under 25 years of age, 80%)
Theft (except auto)	55.0%	(under 25 years of age, 76%)
Auto theft	62.0%	(under 25 years of age, 88%)[18]

These percentage figures do not represent a new trend in crime; throughout history most crime has been committed by the under twenty-five year-old age group.[19]

Sex Groups

Which sex has the highest arrest frequency? Chart III indicates that males are arrested for criminal offenses six times more frequently than women. The highest category for males is larceny which amounts to almost 50% of their total arrests for all categories. Females are also arrested more often for larceny, which accounts for 75% of their total arrests for all categories.

Chart III. TOTAL ARRESTS, DISTRIBUTION BY SEX, 1966

CRIME	TOTAL	MALE	FEMALE
PROPERTY:			
Burglary	199,781	192,085	7,696
Auto Theft	105,778	101,462	4,316
Larceny	398,623	306,727	91,896
PERSONAL:			
Homicide	10,734	9,092	1,642
Robbery	47,031	44,682	2,349
Aggravated Assault	98,406	85,433	12,973
Forcible Rape	11,609	11,609	- - - - -

Figures taken from *Uniform Crime Reports in the United States, 1966,* p. 117. These figures are based on statistics from 4,042 agencies; 1966 estimated population 137,986,000.

Ethnic Groups

According to Chart IV nonwhite arrests numbered 283,880 while Caucasians had almost two arrests (520,792) for every nonwhite arrest.

However, the population in the United States as of October 1, 1966, was 196,417,000, of which 23,589,000 were nonwhite. Ninety-two percent (21,511,000) of the nonwhite population was Negro.[20] The fact that there were approximately eight

---

[18]Beattie and Kenney, *op. cit.,* pp. 73-85.

[19]*Loc. cit.*

[20]Jean Paradise, & Maron Loeb et al, Editors, *Collier's 1967 Year Book Covering The Year 1966* (Crowell Collier and Macmillian, Inc., United States of America, 1967), p. 600.

Caucasians for every nonwhite in the United States in 1966 partially explains the seemingly high Caucasian arrest rates. The arrest figures could be easily misinterpreted unless the total population figure for each category is known.

Chart IV. TOTAL ARRESTS, DISTRIBUTION BY RACE, 1966

CRIME	TOTAL	CAUCASIAN	NEGRO	INDIAN	CHINESE	JAPANESE	OTHERS
PROPERTY:							
Burglary	187,642	125,512	58,688	1,200	55	164	2,023
Auto Theft	97,795	68,554	26,985	953	27	104	1,172
Larceny	383,378	262,821	113,906	2,533	259	374	3,485
PERSONAL:							
Homicide	9,911	5,091	4,639	87	2	7	85
Robbery	40,671	16,505	23,451	336	11	18	350
Aggravated Assault	75,040	37,060	36,723	650	13	34	560
Forcible Rape	10,235	5,249	4,806	68	2	1	109
Subtotal for above arrests	804,672	520,792	269,198	5,827	369	702	7,784

Figures taken from *Uniform Crime Reports in the United States, 1966,* p. 119. These figures are based on statistics reported from only 4,021 agencies serving an estimated population of 128,163,000 in 1966.

COST OF CRIME

Surface Cost

Although you may never become the personal victim of a crime, you cannot escape the surface, hidden, or related costs of crime. Crime prevention, the destruction due to crime, and the rehabilitation of criminals cost Americans over sixty million dollars per day,[21] above twenty billion annually, or seven percent of the national income.[22] For example, ten percent of New York City's $5.18 billion 1967 operating budget was spent in fighting crime in an effort to make the streets of the nation's largest city safer for law-abiding citizens. New York City's 10% budget exceeded California's budget by $120 million dollars.[23] When crime rate is compared to the population of cities, Los Angeles has eight times as many reported crimes as New York City.[24]

Destruction and property loss due to burglaries, auto thefts, robberies, and larcenies exceeded one billion dollars in the United States in 1966.[25] Thefts by drug addicts alone cost the citizens of Los Angeles about $200,000.00 per day.[26] These astronomical figures refer to surface costs. In addition, there are hidden and related costs.

[21]Judge Sherman G. Finesilver, "Justice", *Vital Speeches,* XXVI (May 19, 1960), p. 669.

[22]J. Edgar Hoover, "An American's Callenge", *Vital Speeches,* XXIX (December 1, 1962), p. 99.

[23]*Los Angeles Times* (June 4, 1967), Section A, p. 1.

[24]"The Safest Large City", *American City,* LXXX (August, 1965), p. 160.

[25]"New Evidence of the Terrific Spurt of Crime in America", *U.S. News and World Report,* LXIII (August 21, 1967), p. 12.

[26]Los Angeles County Board of Supervisors, *Darkness On Your Doorstep* (Los Angeles, California, Matthews Rotary Press, 1966), p. 10.

Hidden Cost

The hidden costs for the investigation of even a small burglary include the following procedures: time for the manager to talk to officers, inventory and paper work for clerks, time lost while clerks are discussing the burglary, time spent by clerk sending forms to the insurance company to file claim, cost to replace stolen items, time for manager to go to court, and transportation to and from court hearings.[27]

Related Cost

Related crime costs include imprisonment and rehabilitation costs. The total operational costs for an adult committed to The California Department of Corrections is $4,700 per year, and $150 per year for supervision under parole.[28] Over seventy-five percent of the offenders are repeaters; consequently, society continues to pay expenses for many of the same criminals over and over.[29]

SUMMARY

The value of crime statistics depends upon the accuracy, interpretation, and application of the data. The reliability of crime statistics improves yearly. Ironically, as the tools and methodology of compilation improve and make possible more accurate data, the possibility of misinterpretation increases; comparisons of crime rates from year to year or decade to decade often fail to account for the improved compilation.

Experts — not headline writers — must interpret statistics on crime. Factors which influence the findings must be considered. For instance, crime arrest data suggests that white males under twenty-five have the highest arrest rate. However, the white population is eight times greater than the nonwhite population, and the under twenty-five age group constitutes approximately fifty percent of the total population.[30] Therefore, to be accurate any statement about the arrest rate must include the population factors.

The average taxpaying citizen needs no statistics to tell him that crime costs are rising. Nevertheless, crime statistics can provide an intelligent basis for assessing the value of such programs as imprisonment and rehabilitation. Crime statistics reflect the problems; society and the citizen, the victims of criminal behavior, must solve the problems.

[27]Philip H. Ennis, *Criminal Victimization In The United States: A Report Of A National Survey,* University of Chicago National Opinion Research Center (Washington, D.C., U.S. Government Printing Office, May, 1967), pp. 15-16.

[28]Richard A. McGee, *Probation Supervision And Training* (Sacramento, California, Board of Corrections, 1964), p. 14.

[29]"Crime Runs Wild — Will It Be Halted?" *U.S. News and World Report,* LIX (August 9, 1965), pp. 64-67.

[30]Luman H. Long, editor, *World Almanac 1967* (New York Newspaper Enterprise Inc., World Almanac Division, 1966), p. 326.

Chapter Three

FACTORS
THAT INFLUENCE CRIME

INTRODUCTION

The preceding chapters based on crime statistics indicate that criminal behavior is a growing problem in our society. If the criminal statistics are to do more than create fear and astonishment, they must be used to help us understand *why* criminal behavior occurs and *how* it can be deterred and eventually eliminated. According to crime statistics young adults, urban-dwellers, and males all have comparatively high crime rates. What conditions or factors influence each group separately? Are any conditions or factors common to all three groups which would account for their criminal behavior?

The greatest difficulty in arriving at a satisfactory causal theory of crime is the fact that the same conditions do not cause the same response by different individuals. For instance, all poor, badly housed, central city, young males of broken families do not engage in criminal behavior. Therefore, it cannot be said that these conditions cause crime.

Behavior is a learned response; criminal behavior is also learned. What are the learning conditions? Economic status, education, and religion are repeatedly proposed as interrelated community variables which can establish conditions to deter or encourage criminal behavior by the individual.

ECONOMIC STATUS

Economic status is a complex of variable factors such as housing, health, education, and social status. The low economic status of poverty is often manifested in poor housing conditions and poor health. Poverty-stricken individuals usually have low social status. They often have little to lose, little to respect, and very little incentive to work toward self-advancement. In many cases both parents work; the children spend most of their time unsupervised, and often the parents are fatigued and irritable when they are home. These conditions often lead the child to drop out of school at the earliest permissible age in order to enter unskilled occupations which may be uninteresting and offer little opportunity for advancement and remuneration.

Within the low economic class the ratio of criminal offenses varies by social group. For example, children in a Japanese colony in Seattle prior to World War II had very low delinquency rates despite the fact that they were as poverty-stricken as residents of the surrounding area who had high rates. Since the same degree of poverty did not result in the same degree of delinquency, other factors such as family and cultural ethics must account for their behavior. Other studies indicate that, "In some situations working class people have crime rates lower than those of other classes."[31]

---

[31]Edwin H. Sutherland and Donald R. Cressey, *Principles of Criminology,* 7th. Edition (Philadelphia, J.B. Lippincott Company, 1966), p. 237.

As the example above illustrates, information about economic status and crime rates is inconclusive and contradictory. Most studies indicate that there is a higher ratio for crimes against property, such as larceny and burglary, committed by unskilled workers. However, a Detroit study indicated that unskilled workers do not commit as many auto thefts as others. [32]

Besides sociological factors affecting crimes committed, differences in arresting practices for lower socio-economic class people tend to exaggerate crime rates for this group. It is important to note that statistics based on sociological classification are generally biased by the exclusion of white-collar crime. White-collar crime is a violation of law by respected business and professional people. White-collar crime is usually thought of as involving only the theft of articles from the place of employment. However, there are various types of white-collar crimes; a large percentage of these crimes involve (1) misrepresentation of asset values and (2) duplicity in the manipulation of power. "The first is approximately the same as fraud or swindling; the second is similiar to the double-cross." [33] Since most white-collar crime is not reported and not prosecuted, it is real crime. Therefore, statistical figures for such are low.

To conclude, it is inaccurate to claim that poverty alone influences crime, or to claim that statistics show accurately how much more, if any, crime is committed by the lower economic classes than by other economic groups.

EDUCATION

The school, like the family, is a community institution and does not exist in isolation from other sociological forces. Its location and the economic status of the community may determine the possibilities for education, the type of curriculum, the quality of instruction, and the scope of the social program.

High truancy rates are generally characteristic of the school located in a low economic community. There is a high correlation between truancies, drop-outs, and delinquent behavior. One study concerning juveniles involved in thefts showed that 60% were habitual truants. [34] The economic status of the residents in a given locality also has a bearing on the frequency of delinquency in a given school. However, the boy from a low socio-economic class is less likely to become delinquent if he is a member of a minority group in the school and residential community. [35] The attitudes and behavior of the majority ethnic group may exert a strong influence upon the boy to emulate them. Then, too, school as such has less influence than its students. For example, if the school population is made up of students from a high delinquency area, it is difficult to reduce the delinquency simply by the school's efforts to instill anti-criminal attitudes. [36]

RELIGION

The effect of religion on behavior is perhaps the most difficult to assess because it is personal and psychological. Its influence may be nominal, practical, or irrelevant.

Lack of religious training is often blamed as the cause of crime because the church is held responsible for teaching members of society to behave morally. However, there

[32]*Ibid.,* p. 238.

[33]Edwin H. Sutherland, "White Collar Criminality," in *Mass Society In Crisis,* Bernard Rosenberg, Israel Gerver, F. William Howton (New York, The Macmillian Company, 1964), pp. 35-37.

[34]Sutherland and Cressey, *op. cit.,* p. 252.

[35]Albert J. Reiss, Jr. and Albert Lewis Rhodes, "The Distribution of Juvenile Delinquency in the Social Class Structure," *American Sociological Review,* XXVI (October, 1961), pp. 720-732.

[36]Sutherland and Cressey, *op. cit.,* p. 252.

is insufficient evidence to correlate lack of religious training with criminal behavior.[37]

Two Catholic priests studying 45 adult prisoners found that 87% of the prisoners indicated some religious affiliation while only about 40% of the general population at that time expressed religious affiliation.[38] Some prisons in the United States do not report religious affiliation; those that do report indicate that the Baptists and Catholics have the highest rate of criminal commitments.[39] As in the previous study, the extent to which these prisoners practiced their religion, or how often they attended church services, is not known.

Another study indicates that delinquents have more favorable attitudes than do non-delinquents toward the religious issues of Sunday observance, the Bible, and war. Carmen V. Diaz in a study involving 915 girls in religious instruction classes found the subject matter itself inappropriate in helping the student apply religious principles of moral law to life situations.[41]

Stating, then, that the cause of crime is related to a lack of religious training is misleading because of insufficient proof.

SUMMARY

Economic status, education, and religion - interrelated community variables - may or may not influence the individual's behavior. Whether community conditions influence the person toward social or anti-social behavior depends in part upon the individual's personal psychological development, since patterns of behavior are initially learned through interpersonal relations with one's family, peers, and authority figures, who in turn have learned their behavior patterns under personal and community conditions. Thus, past personal and social conditioning flow into the present and influence the future.

Although the evidence does not support a statement that poverty, lack of education, or lack of religious training results in criminal behavior, common sense indicates that to be deprived of the things most prized by society damages the individual's respect for self and the society. Until these relationships are clarified, society cannot identify the causes of criminal behavior; therefore, society and the individual must concentrate their efforts on combating crime.

[37]*Ibid.*, p. 248.

[38]*Ibid.*, p. 249.

[39]Philip M. Smith, "Organized Religion and Criminal Behavior," *Sociology and Social Research*, XXXIII (May, 1949), pp. 362-367.

[40]Sutherland and Cressey, *op. cit.*, p. 248.

[41]Carmen V. Diaz, *A Study of the Ability of Eleventh Grade Girls to Apply the Principles of Moral Law to Actual and Hypothetical Life Situations* (unpublished Ph.D. Dissertation, Fordham, University, 1952).

Chapter Four

CURRENT TRENDS
IN
COMBATING CRIME

INTRODUCTION

Crime, like a multiplying cancer cell, has invaded our society. Unable to identify and eliminate the causes, we are forced to treat the symptoms. In response to this spreading violence and crime, a war against crime is currently being waged by official agencies in all branches of the local, state, and federal governments. New weapons and tactics are being developed and employed. Among them are law enforcement education and legislation, which can be implemented if appropriations are provided.

LAW ENFORCEMENT EDUCATION

In 1964 the President of the United States by proclamation established May 1 as LAW DAY. Certainly the proclamation has not deterred crime, but the need for a proclamation does illustrate the seriousness of the crime problem in our society.

Law enforcement education programs seek to combat and eliminate criminal behavior. The auxiliary police force program aids in the arrest of persons who have committed crimes. The police-youth counseling program attempts to prevent behavior that could lead to arrest.

Auxiliary Police Force

One of the most difficult problems in combating crime is obtaining arrests. Victims and witnesses do not report offenses because they do not think the acts are police matters; they do not feel the police would be effective; they do not wish to be involved; or they fear reprisal.[42]

To combat this problem several Chicago business firms enlisted their employees and individual citizens to become members of an auxiliary police force. The auxiliary members were provided with a wallet card telling them exactly what to do when they saw something suspicious. Listed on the card was a special telephone number to call. Members of the auxiliary police force were aware of the fact that under this new alert system a squad car could be on the scene thirty seconds after they reported an incident. As a result, a dramatic increase in obtaining arrests was achieved.

Police-Youth Counseling

Statistics reveal that young people commit more criminal offenses than any other age group. Because of this, attention is now being given to junior and senior high school

[42]Ennis, *op. cit.,* p. 45.

students before they develop the will to commit a crime. Some schools provide office space within the school building for a resource police officer. Students who are most likely to start trouble are singled out by school personnel and referred to the officer. The police officer holds conferences with these students and has them accompany him on a tour of duty in order to explain some of the community problems and types of cases handled. The program helps the students understand the role and function of the police force. This is a relatively new program; consequently, its effect on crime rate is unknown, but all available reports seem favorable.[43]

LEGISLATION

Firearms

The assassination of President John F. Kennedy with a mail-order rifle offered a grim and tragic illustration of what can result when firearms are easily available to anyone in the United States.

Federal control of firearms is limited by the second amendment, which provides that ". . . a well-regulated militia, being necessary to the security of the free State, the right of the people to keep and bear Arms shall not be infringed."[44]

Evaluation of the effectiveness of a comprehensive national plan for the control of firearms is at best speculative in the absence of such a scheme. The widely varying state laws present no obstacle for the determined purchaser; if he is restricted in his own state, he may simply drive to a neighboring state and there purchase the weapon he desires. Furthermore, it is almost impossible to curb the sometimes unscrupulous mail-order firms which send firearms in unmarked packages. "Massachusetts and New York, the two states with strict controls in effect over a long period of time, report 35.3 and 31.8 respectively as the percentage of murders by firearms; Georgia and Texas, two states with very few controls, report percentages of 66.6 and 68.7."[45] This evidence would seem to indicate that strict firearms legislation is of significant value in reducing the number of homicides by firearms.

Wiretapping

Wiretapping became a public issue early in the twentieth century when the development of mechanical and electronic devices enabled a third party to secretly overhear and record conversations transmitted over a telephone wire.[46]

As stated in the Legislative Reference Service Report, *Combating Crime in the United States,*

> "Federal law ostensibly prohibits wiretapping and divulgence of intercepted communications. The power of Congress to enact such laws has been sustained even with regard to intrastate wire communications which form part of an interstate network. Wiretap evidence is inadmissible in the federal courts by virtue of the supervisory power of the Supreme Court over the federal judicial system; but the same evidence is not inadmissible in the state courts under federal law, even though disclosure of such evidence in state courts is technically a federal crime. However, despite the well-known prohibitions against it, there is reason to believe that wiretapping is widely practiced by both private individuals and state and federal officers."[47]

[43]Committee on the Judiciary United States Senate Ninetieth Congress First Session, *Controlling Crime Through More Effective Law Enforcement* (Washington, D.C., U.S. Government Printing Office, 1967), p. 372.

[44]Legislative Reference Service, Library of Congress, *Combating Crime In The United States,* 90th. Congress, First Session, Senate, Document No. 26 (Washington, D.C., U.S. Government Printing Office, May 1967), p. 183.

[45]*Ibid,* p. 185.

[46]*Ibid,* p. 32.

[47]*Ibid.,* pp. 47-48.

The use of wiretaps to obtain information about suspected criminal activities has resulted in a legislative and judicial problem. Opponents state that wiretapping violates citizen rights guaranteed by the Constitution. The innocent and the suspect are denied their rights of privacy, freedom of expression, and protection from self-incrimination.

President Johnson responded to public criticism over government wiretapping practices and issued an executive order for all federal agencies except the Justice Department to cease all such activities in July, 1965. Consequently, wiretapping may be practiced by the Justice Department, but only in cases involving national security. The Justice Department must also secure permission from the Attorney General before the actual tap is done. President Johnson's executive order restricting wiretapping applies only to national officials; consequently, state and local police officers are not affected.[48]

Several states that prohibit wiretaps do not apply their laws to state police officers acting in their official capacity. Likewise, federal officials have been allowed to wiretap in states with statutes that prohibit it. New York, Maryland, Massachusetts, Nevada, and Oregon have laws or constitutional provisions allowing wiretapping by police officers if they secure prior written permission from a state court. Thirty-three states have statutes that prohibit wiretapping while eleven states have no laws regarding wiretapping.[49]

Statistics employed to illustrate a real need for wiretapping are inconclusive.[50] Most of the convictions based on the utilization of wiretapping involve moral law, such as abortion and prostitution as well as bookmaking, gambling, and vice. There appear to be no data regarding the indispensability of wiretapping in the convictions that have been obtained through its use.[51]

It is clear that wiretapping of telephones is a dangerous threat to freedom because one may incrimate himself unknowingly, have his privacy invaded, or be held responsible for expressions he would not have used so freely had he known his conversation was not private.

Future statutes must limit wiretapping to specific circumstances to avoid jeopardizing the personal liberties of our citizens. It must be shown that effective law enforcement in an appreciable number of cases would be impossible without this method. According to available data, wiretapping is basically ineffective in combating crime.[52]

Right Of Self-Defense

Under present laws and court decisions, law enforcement agencies claim extreme difficulties in successfully apprehending and convicting criminals. Mounting pressures demand that legislators take action in combating crime. One of the most important domestic political issues in the 1968 election campaigns is the issue of crime deterrence.

In January, 1968, the New York State Commission on Review of the Penal Law recommended that the New York legislature grant police and private citizens the power to shoot to kill those who have committed a felony or are suspected of having committed a felony.

New York's current law allows citizens to use deadly force only where there is definite reason to believe that the intruder would use physical force. In order to be certain beyond any reasonable doubt that bodily harm may be inflicted on the victim by the

[48]*Ibid.*, p. 34.
[49]*Loc. cit.*
[50]*Ibid.*, p. 57.
[51]*Ibid.*, p. 56.
[52]*Ibid.*, p. 58.

criminal, the victim is sometimes forced into waiting and trying to anticipate the actions of his assailant. Placed at this serious disadvantage, the victim loses the opportunity for self-defense.

Under the new recommendation the police would be given the right to shoot or use deadly force (without fear of later recrimination) in apprehending anyone attempting to escape from custody, anyone believed to be committing a kidnap, arson, or armed burglary.

Even more important, the commission recommended that private citizens fearing physical harm by an intruder in their homes, apartments or elsewhere be permitted to use deadly force without later recrimination.[53]

The significant implication of this proposed law lies in the word "fear". The victim need only fear bodily harm in order to utilize deadly force against an attacker at any time or in any palce, rather than waiting to be certain beyond any doubt that bodily harm may be inflicted.

The mere fact that the State Commission has submitted this bill to the legislature in no way assures the success of its passage. There will be opposition undoubtedly from legislative members and attorneys who specialize in the defense of criminal cases.[54]

APPROPRIATIONS

Central to the legislative debate is the question of cost. Will the sharp increase in budget for combating crime, though expensive, be worthwhile? Proponents of additional expenditures for crime control must consider how these additional funds can be best spent. "Eighty-five to ninety percent of the current $4 billion-a-year budget for public law enforcement represents salaries for policemen. If we decide to invest in more police-men, will we be happy with the costly intrusion of authority into our lives? Who would choose to live in a garrison city in which policemen and guards are always in sight on every corner and in every park? Over-enforcement entails, in addition to heavy costs in terms of public disrespect for basic rules, the encouragement of organized crime."[55]

Therefore, if funds are increased, it is extremely important that they be used for innovation and improvement of all agencies and not be earmarked for the police only, or dissipated in new buildings, salaries, or standard equipment alone.

SUMMARY

The war against crime is limited warfare; the current trends in combating crime are limited efforts. Both the auxiliary police force and the police-youth counseling programs are virtually untried because they require more personnel and more money than have been made available. Firearms legislation faces strong opposition by lobbyists, and wire-tap legislation is a confusion of constitutional questions.

The solution to the current crime problem lies not so much in anti-crime measures, but in the citizen's will and effort to destroy the causes of crime. To understand the causes of criminal behavior, crime statistics must become more accurate and be intelli-gently interpreted and applied. The war against crime, like the war against poverty, has not been won and will not be won until the conditions influencing crime have been

---

[53]Caspar W. Weinberger, "New York Proposal To Loosen Police Curbs Has Merit", *Los Angeles Times* (February 2, 1968), Part II, p. 5, Column 1-2.

[54]*Loc. cit.*

[55]Arthur Rosett, "Topical Comment: Crime Crackdown, A Necessary But Expensive Project", *Los Angeles Times* (January 21, 1968), Section G, p. 7, Columns 3-5.

destroyed. In the meantime the individual must assume the responsibility for her own safety. Each person must learn how to avoid becoming a victim of property and personal crime. The rest of this book will demonstrate how personal protection and self-defense can be made to work for you.

PART II

PROPERTY SAFETY

Chapter Five

DEVICES

INTRODUCTION

Since earliest times man has felt the need to protect his dwelling and possessions from intruders. In ancient times man rolled a boulder in front of the cave entrance, or a medicine man cast the evil spirits away from a man's door. Through the centuries excellent lock and alarm systems have been invented. Yet, last year 1,370,300 burglaries were reported in the United States.[56] The safety of property persists as one of man's basic worries and responsibilities. In today's urban and mobile civilization in which neighbors are often strangers and burglars can operate unnoticed, the individual can protect his property with effective locks, alarms, and keys.

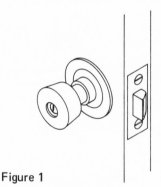

Figure 1

LOCKS

The prices, qualities, and types of locks are numerous. Unfortunately for the layman the price of a lock is not a satisfactory criterion for judging the security a lock will provide. Rather, the effectiveness of a lock depends upon how it operates. The following discussion of types of locks proceeds from the least protective to the most protective.

Although not guaranteed for even minimum safety, the most common house and apartment lock is the spring or snap lock (see Figure 1). The lock can be set by pushing in or turning the button located in the center of the doorknob, or pushing in and turning the whole doorknob. When the door is closed, the latch snaps into a metal strike plate on the doorjamb and locks the door. It is inexpensive and easy to operate; however, it is also unsafe. It is a simple operation for a burglar to slide a strip of celluloid, a wire, a filed down screwdriver, a playing card, or a knive blade between the doorjamb and the metal strike plate to push back the latch. Because the keyhole is in the doorknob, a burglar can fix a pipe wrench on the doorknob and quickly twist it open.

---

[56]J. Edgar Hoover, *Uniform Crime Reports in the United States, 1966* (Washington, D.C., U.S. Government Printing Office, 1967), p. 15.

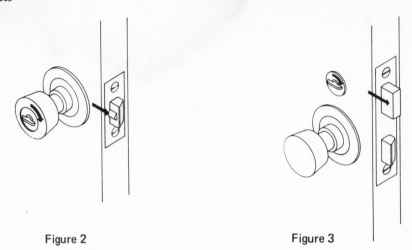

Figure 2   Figure 3

Most spring locks are now manufactured with a small trigger guard directly adjacent to the latch (see Figure 2). The trigger fits into a hole in the metal strike plate and guards the spring latch so it cannot be forced out of the strike plate. However, if there is a gap along the edge of the doorjamb, a burglar can easily jimmy the latch out of the strike plate.

One of the better and certainly safer locks for outside doors is the dead bolt lock (see Figure 3). It is operated with a key or knob, and cannot be opened with a knife, playing card, or wire because the bolt that inserts into the strike plate is long and square shaped, not short and tapered like a spring latch.

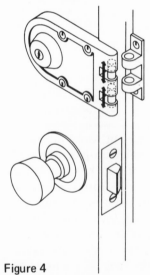

Figure 4

The Segal-type lock, manufactured by several companies, is the most force-resistant dead bolt lock on the market (see Figure 4). It has two bolts that slip vertically into metal hasps which are attached to the doorjamb. It is important that the screws which fasten the metal hasp to the doorjamb be at least one inch long to insure the security of the lock against force.[57]

[57]Joe Alex Morris, "How To Lock Burglars Out", *Reader's Digest*, LXXXIX (December 1966), pp. 137-140.

Chain locks, if installed properly, are very good for a second lock. The bracket from which the chain hangs when the lock is not in use must be attached to the doorjamb or anchored into a heavy beam with at least one inch screws. To test the lock from the outside to be certain the chain is not too long, slip your hand through the opening and try to unhook the chain. If the chain can be released, remove several links until the chain fits the lock properly. Be sure the chain is of heavy-duty links similar to motor-cycle chain which is available in most hardware stores. If you do not have a porthole or window near your door, use the chain lock when opening the door to a caller. When a door has a dead bolt lock and a chain lock, a burglar cannot get in unless he tears the whole doorjamb off. This involves too much risk because the splinter of wood can sound like a gun shot.

Police locks are safe locks and are slightly more expensive than a dead bolt lock because of the installation fee. Police locks are available in two styles; one can be used only from the inside, the other may be used from either side.

Both styles have a socket built inside the lower portion of the door. From this socket a rod is released which inserts and locks into a steel plate that is permanently installed in the floor.[58]

All patio and terrace doors should have strong, secure locks. Some sliding glass doors are now available with police locks. The chance of entry by breaking the glass and un-locking sliding glass doors can be reduced by having tempered, Herculite, or wire-mesh glass installed.[59]

Sargent and Company has a lock for about $50.00 that offers superb security. The lock with twelve pins arranged in three rows is opened with a special key that cannot be duplicated except in the factory under top security conditions. The key does not look like an ordinary serrated key, but rather has precise milled depressions in both side surfaces and on one edge. The innovation of this lock is that it provides fifty times as many key combinations as an ordinary lock and cannot be opened by using a lock pick.[60]

Another new lock is a keyless, push-button combination lock which costs $15.00 to $20.00. Each lock has 1100 combination possibilities. At any time the owner of such a lock may set his own combination in about one minute. There are other multi-com-bination locks that work on a dial principle similar to that of a telephone.[61]

Even the best lock will not protect your dwelling and possessions if the windows are not secured. Small window locks and keys cost about $2.00 and are widely available. These locks allow the window to be opened about four inches for ventilation and pre-vent a burglar from opening it wide enough to enter. Sash windows are secured by screw-ing a metal block in the window track in a position that allows the window to be opened only a few inches for ventilation.

Sliding horizontal windows can be removed easily and silently by any burglar if they are not kept locked. Place a thin metal rod the length of the window into the track that the window slides along when opening. A hole should be drilled near one end of the rod for placement of a screw so the rod can be removed when you want the window open for ventilation (see Figure 5).

A good lock decreases the probability of victimization by a burglar by discouraging the burglar's attempt altogether, or by slowing him down long enough for the incident to be reported and the burglar apprehended.

[58]Accas and Eckstein, *op. cit.,* p. 12.

[59]*Ibid.,* p. 14.

[60]Morris, *op. cit.,* p. 138.

[61]*Ibid.,* p. 139.

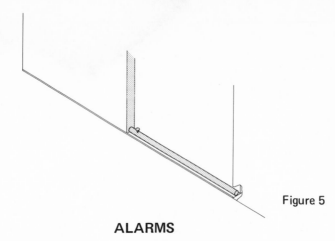

Figure 5

ALARMS

For added protection in the event the lock system fails, an alarm system may be installed. Women may increase their security by purchasing a noisy dog or installing an alarm system. Battery operated alarms that are placed over the door cost from $12.00 to $15.00. When the owner of such an alarm goes out or retires for the night, he merely sets the alarm mechanism to the on-position. A loud alarm begins to ring thirty seconds after the door is opened allowing the owner sufficient time to turn the alarm off if he is the person opening the door.[62] A quick, attentive burglar may likewise see the alarm and shut it off. A better alarm is one that can be turned off only with a key, which prevents the burglar from turning off the loud piercing sound even if he does find the alarm.

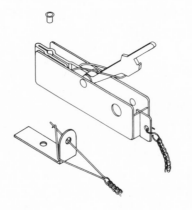

Figure 6

Another alarm that will give any burglar a frightful scare is a device called Burglar Alarm that uses a primer which sounds like a gun shot when triggered (see Figure 6). Burglar Alarm can be attached to any surface no matter how rough, greasy, or irregular. It can be located so that opening the door, window, patio door, or garage will fire the alarm (see Figures 7-10). Burglar Alarm costs $2.95, and replacement primers can be obtained from most sporting goods stores for a nominal charge.

[62]*Ibid.*, p. 140.

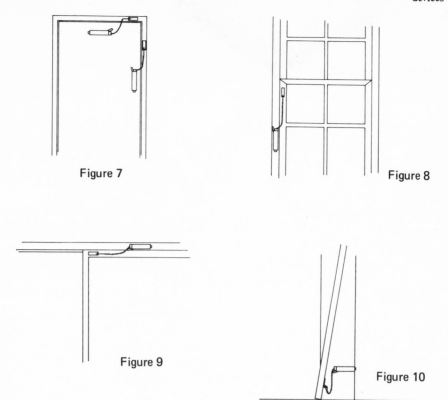

Figure 7

Figure 8

Figure 9

Figure 10

If you do have a burglar alarm system, however, show your close neighbors how the mechanism operates so they will recognize the sound and will telephone the police upon hearing it. Never play with the alarm; do not show every guest who visits you how it operates. Neighbors will ignore the sound your alarm system makes if you are continually playing with it.

Fire alarms put out by EMDKO can also be used as burglar alarms. These alarms cost about $200.00 for a set of eight, an alarm for each room in the house. Example of possible use: victim, hearing a strange noise in the living room after retiring for the night, quietly reaches up and turns the manual knob on the fire alarm. The sharp penetrating sound will likely scare the burglar away and attract the attention of neighbors.

Investment in a buglar alarm may be wisely spent dollars giving you peace of mind, protecting your valuables, and perhaps saving your life.

KEYS

Since the majority of lock systems consist of a lock and key, the best lock system is vulnerable if the key is not safeguarded. One of the principal reasons for loss of security is the ease with which ordinary keys can be duplicated.

In old and new buildings many unknown persons may have duplicate keys. In a brand new house as many as ten duplicate keys may have been issued to such persons as the building contractor, real estate agent, cabinet maker, carpet layer, electrician, plumber, painter, et cetera — any of whom could have had copies made. Before moving into a different house or apartment, the individual should employ a reputable locksmith to change the locks or reset the tumblers in a pin type lock.

Regulations governing the licensing of locksmiths vary from state to state. Some states require the individual who wishes to become a locksmith to attend special classes to become familiar with various kinds of locks and to pass a written state examination. A few states require that the locksmith be bondable and/or pass a written state examination. Other states, including California, have no laws at all concerning the licensing of locksmiths; anyone can become a locksmith merely by paying a $10.00 fee. If you move to an unfamiliar town or city and want to employ a reputable locksmith to change or install a new lock, telephone the local police department and ask them for the name and address of a reputable locksmith. If you find it necessary to have your keys duplicated, watch the locksmith to be certain that he does not duplicate a key for himself.

SUMMARY

Locks, alarms, and keys are the most common, mechanical devices used to provide property protection. The amount of protection depends upon the type and quality of the lock or alarm. However, the best locks are vulnerable if the keys or combinations are not safeguarded. It is absolutely essential that a new lock system be installed if you lose your key or move into a different or new dwelling. The expense and bother of installation is a nuisance, but the expense and bother of a burglary could be an emotional and financial catastrophe.

Chapter Six

PRECAUTIONS

INTRODUCTION

Property protection is not completely assured by lock and alarm devices; unfortunately, amateur and professional burglars often succeed simply because of the victims' ignorance or carelessness. Whenever duplicate keys are distributed indiscriminately, doors are left unlocked, or vacations are announced in the social pages of the newspapers, burglary is encouraged. The potential victim is an inadvertent accomplice of the criminal. For example, the following incident shows how Mrs. Greene's carelessness aided a criminal.

One evening about 9:00 p.m. a burglar spotted a dark house. He briskly walked to the front door and rang the bell; when no one answered, he went around to the kitchen door in the back of the house. Posted on the kitchen door was a note to the milkman that read, "We have gone to Florida — please discontinue our milk delivery from December 20 till the 3rd of January. Mrs. Greene." This message indicated to the burglar that the Greenes would be away for five more days. He jimmied the back door, packed up all the small items, books, pictures, ashtrays, knick-knacks, bedding, and clothing and took it all home with him. The next day the burglar telephoned three used furniture dealers and told them he was moving to Florida and wanted to sell all his furniture. All three agencies sent a dealer; by 11:00 a.m. the dealers had finished bidding against each other and all the furniture was sold.

To reduce the risk of becoming the victim of a burglar, the individual must take precautionary measures, such as caring for keys and preparing the dwelling for brief or extended vacancies. Common sense and an awareness of the professional burglar's procedures are the basis for effective counter-measures.

KEY CARE

Key care is the conscious effort to discard habits which jeopardize property safety. Because keys open locks, they are a convenient necessity but also a possible danger to the security of property. The practice of issuing duplicate house or apartment keys to acquaintances, milk, laundry or grocery delivery services should be avoided. It is equally risky to inform such people of the hiding place for duplicates as burglars can observe and gain entrance the same way.

Duplicate house, apartment, and automobile keys for the owner's emergency use should be kept in a safe place. Avoid "hiding" house keys under the door-mat, on a nail near the door, under a porch ornament, or in a joist that serves as a roof brace. These common "hiding" places are known to everyone including burglars.

Hiding duplicate car keys is a greater challenge because the car is mobile. Never place duplicates in a metal magnetic box attached under the fender, hood, or bumper. Car thieves look in those places first. Keep an extra key in your wallet or at home. If it is kept at home, the car may be some distance away when the key is needed, but inconvenience is a small price to pay for the safekeeping of your automobile.

Precautions must be taken with regular sets of keys also. Never carry house and car keys on the same key ring. Often car keys must be left in the car when parking in public lots, providing an opportunity for house keys to be duplicated. Avoid placing automobile license number and name and address identification tags on the key chain or ring. License number tags may be convenient for individuals unable to memorize their license numbers, but, if the keys are lost, the numbers are extremely convenient for the finder.

Except when prohibited in public parking lots, lock your car and carry the keys with you even for stops of brief duration. Never leave your keys in the ignition, under the seat, over the visor, or in the glove box. Over forty percent of auto thefts occurring in 1966 had keys left in the ignition, or the ignitions were left unlocked.[63] Key care will make the auto thief's and burglar's work more difficult and less successful.

BURGLAR PROCEDURES

Professional burglars make their living off their victims' carelessness. The following description of the burglar's procedures provides insight and a basis for counter-measures which will protect home and property at night and during evening and vacation absences.

The working hours for most professional house burglars are from just before dark until 10:30 to 11:00 p.m. Too much risk is involved in burglarizing a home after 11:00 p.m. because the people may have come home and gone to bed. The professional takes every precaution possible to avoid coming in contact with people inside the dwelling being burglarized. Considerable planning takes place before the professional will attempt to "knock over" a place. Sometimes a house is cased for several weeks before the job is attempted. Casing the potential burglar site allows the professional to learn the occupants' habits; such as, what time the people leave for work, the day grocery shopping is done, the time the children come and go, et cetera.

Although the following description of a professional house thief consistently describes a male, the profession of house breaking is not limited exclusively to the male sex.

The professional usually drives a fairly new car and dresses well in a dark business suit or perhaps a white dinner jacket. The professional drives to a wealthy neighborhood and parks the car in front of a row of three or four houses that have no lights. One house is then selected, and the address along with a fake name is written in the professional's address book. He may carry a camera, briefcase, vacuumn cleaner, flowers, or other items to disguise himself as having a legitimate business. The professional burglar walks boldly to the front door and rings the bell several times. If the lights come on and someone answers the door, he asks if John Dokes is at home? When the occupant replies, "No one by that name lives here", the professional quickly looks in his address book and says, "That's peculiar, I have the address John gave me written down right here." He then politely excuses himself for bothering the would-be-victim. On the other hand, if no lights come on and no one answers the door, the burglar quickly slips a knife blade or filed-down screw driver between the doorjamb and the strike plate; any door with only a spring latch will open immediately. Once inside, the professional opens the back door and a window away from the garage side of the house to provide three possible exits should anyone return home before he completes the job. The first spot the burglar hits is the linen closet in search of pillow cases to stuff with small items such as cameras, radios, clock, silverware, electrical appliances like a toaster, waffle iron, or egg beater.

[63]*Los Angeles Times* (January 29, 1968), Part II, p. 5, Columns 3-4.

Money, the next item, can often be found in a sugar bowl, coffee can, fruit jar, desk drawer, hat box, out in the open, in women's lingerie or socks in dresser drawers, stuffed in old shoes or in a metal box in a bottom drawer or on a top shelf.

Jewelry is another important item a burglar looks for. Most professionals will not take jewelry that is out in the open, but rather they look for valuable pieces in a jewelry box and check the small compartments, which is where most people place their most prized jewels.

Once the professional burglar has filled the pillow cases with the items he has selected, he walks calmly back to his car; the pillow cases usually pass for laundry bags, so no one pays much attention.[64]

The efficiency and safety of the professional burglar's methods are illustrated by the arrest rate; only one out of seven burglaries results in arrest.[65]

Because the professional burglar above all else desires to avoid his victims, the chief counter-measure is to give the appearance of being awake during the night and present during brief or extended absences.

COUNTER MEASURES TO TAKE AGAINST THE BURGLAR

Since burglars operate most successfully during the evening and do not wish to encounter inhabitants, special precautions must be taken to outwit the would-be burglar. A light in a dwelling may fool a burglar into believing someone is home. An extremely brave burglar may walk by the side of the house and look in to see if anyone is home. If you have venetian blinds, turn them up so the burglar will be able to see only the ceiling. The best place to leave a light burning in a one story home or apartment is in the bathroom. The bathroom door should be left partially open to permit some light to escape. Turn down the bed covers so that it appears someone has just gotten up and gone into the bathroom.[66] If the house has two stories, leave a light on upstairs. It gives the impression that someone is home, possibly reading in bed, and the burglar cannot look in to be certain that no one is home.

Measures To Take For A Brief Absence And Before Retiring

1. DOORS
    a. Lock garage doors
    b. Latch screen doors
    c. Make sure dutch door is secure
    d. Lock sliding glass doors
    e. Lock basement outside door
    f. Lock accessible door from basement into your house
    g. Set burglar alarm

2. WINDOWS
    a. When you are home, close drapes, curtains, or blinds on windows that face the street to discourage casing.
    b. Check the Burglar Alarm you have set on the one or two windows you regularly leave open for ventilation to be certain it will function properly.
    c. Be sure all accessible windows are locked.

---

[64]Thomas Carter, edited by Robert J. Moskin, "How I'd Rob Your House", *Look Magazine*, XXX (May 31, 1966), pp. 28-29.

[65]Hoover, *op. cit.*, pp. 15 and 117.

[66]Carter and Moskin, *op. cit.*, pp. 28-29.

3.   LIGHTS

    a. Leave at least one night light on inside the house, preferably in the bathroom.

    b. If you use backyard flood lights as a means to discourage burglaries, be sure they are installed so that the light will not shine directly into a neighbor's windows.

4.   OTHERS

    a. Be certain your telephone is in operating order.

    b. Have a list of emergency numbers near the telephone.

    c. Check the flashlight on your night stand to be sure it is in working order.

    d. Keep near your bed a "weapon" you have selected to use for self-defense.

These precautions will protect your property, may give you peaceful slumber, and possibly may save your life.

Measures To Take For An Extended Absence.

1.   Fill out a card at the post office requesting that your mail be forwarded or held until your return.

2.   Telephone the milk company and have the milk delivery discontinued.

3.   Telephone the newspaper office to state the specific dates that delivery service should be discontinued. A pile of newspapers advertises your absence.

4.   Telephone your insurance agent, and for a very nominal fee your fire and theft insurance can be increased for the specific period of your absence.

5.   Telephone the local police department to let them know the length of time you plan to be away and ask them to check your home or apartment on their regular tour of duty.

6.   Telephone the telephone company and have them place your telephone on vacation rates. Vacation rate means that if someone dials your number he will hear the phone ringing. Do not have your telephone temporarily disconnected; for, if the phone has been disconnected, a recording will indicate that fact to all callers. A telephone that is temporarily disconnected suggests that the people may be gone for an extended period of time; whereas a phone on vacation rates rings and merely tells the caller that no one is at home at that moment.

7.   Arrange to have a reliable person tend to the yard work. A burglar may spot your home if the lawn is dry, overgrown, or if there are piles of leaves near your closed garage door. When other yards in the neighborhood are relatively well-kept, your yard may be particularly noticeable if you have not arranged to have someone take care of it while you are away.

8.   Set an automatic light timer in the bathroom or upstairs. The timer costs $5.00 to $7.00 and turns the light on and off at set times. It is never wise to let a light burn continuously while on vacation.

9.   Place any valuable items — papers, jewelry, stamp or coin collections, et cetera — in a safety deposit box in your bank.

10.   Leave some curtains or drapes partially open so that a policeman or neighbor will be able to see the light from a burglar's flashlight.

11.   Tell the landlord where you are going, when you expect to return, and where you can be reached in case of an emergency. You may wish to leave a key to

your apartment with the landlord and have him check your apartment once or twice a week.

12. If you live in a house, tell at least one close neighbor where you are going, when you expect to return, and where you can be reached in case of an emergency.

13. Place a metal rod in all sliding-type doors and windows and be sure they are locked.

14. Set and check the burglar alarm system to be certain it will function properly.

15. Inspect your yard for anything that would attract the attention of a burglar, such as a ladder left leaning up against the side of the house, clothes on a clothes line, children's toys, lawnmower, tractor, garden tools, and patio furniture.

16. List the serial numbers of all your electrical appliances; i.e., radio, television set, vacuumn, coffee pot, egg beater, toaster, and iron in a special booklet. Also list the pattern name of your silverware, china, sterling, and crystal along with the kind and number of each that you own. Keep the booklet in your safety deposit box so you will be able to give details concerning your possessions should your dwelling be burglarized. Most electrical appliances can be recovered if the police know the serial numbers of each item. The burglar usually tries to sell a whole set of china or silverware in one place. If the police are aware of the exact pattern and the specific items missing, they can often trace stolen goods quickly.

SUMMARY

Protecting property from burglary is the responsibility of the owner. The proper use of locks, alarms, and keys and the implementation of anti-burglar measures will safeguard your property and possessions. However, your preparations for property protection must be as conscientious as the professional burglar's are for housebreaking.

PART III

PERSONAL SAFETY

Chapter Seven

TELEPHONE PRECAUTIONS

INTRODUCTION

In the United States today, women enjoy greater freedom than at any other time in our country's history. Second class citizenship for females has been all but abolished. Nearly unlimited opportunities for education, employment, and travel abound; and women have seized these opportunities to participate fully in our society. Today as women move about freely, live alone and travel alone, the crime rate is at its highest, and the streets in many of our cities are unsafe. Self-protection techniques, though not spectacular, are effective means of eliminating or countering dangers that occur while traveling, working, seeking recreation, or simply using a telephone.

Like many other modern conveniences, the telephone can save or endanger human life. It can be used to summon aid, or it can be used to obtain information which may threaten your safety. An apparently harmless remark, such as, "No, my husband won't be home until Friday," can have serious consequences. The following precautions for telephone use are based on discretion born of suspicion.

IDENTIFICATION

Do not reveal your phone number indiscriminately. Always list only your initials and last name in any kind of telephone directory. Never advertise that you are a woman, whether you are a Miss or Mrs. Never print your telephone number on stationery or address stickers.

Be certain that the name on your mailbox does not indicate that you are a woman. Use only your initials and last name. Several kinds of confidence games involve the casing of mailboxes for women who list their names in a manner that makes it obvious that they are women. The name is then matched with their telephone numbers from the public telephone directory. A woman is tailed by a member of the gang to find out where she works, the places she frequents, and as many other details as needed. The woman is then contacted by telephone, and an appointment is arranged under the pretense that she is an heir to a great-uncle's estate, and further identification needs to be made before she can receive X number of dollars. To gain the woman's trust, the member of the confidence gang relates facts concerning where the uncle said she works and frequents. Later he tells her that since the sum is rather large, she could avoid heavy taxation if she had an investment program. He then suggests that she invest $500.00 to $1,000.00 in cash to get her started in an investment program before she recieves the inheritance monies. This is only one example of a swindle that can be made. So, too, the sex criminal, by checking names on mailboxes or looking through public telephone directories, also looks for females who advertise that they are women.

TAKING CALLS

A woman who receives a telephone call for her husband who is out of town should ask who is calling and not reveal that her husband is out of town. Tell a caller that your husband is busy right now, but you would be happy to take a message. If the caller refuses to state his name, sounds mysterious, and will not leave a message, hang up.

If you are a widow and someone telephones and asks to speak to your husband, do not indicate that your husband is dead. Find out who is calling and take a message. Always check out the identity of the caller after you hang up. Never rely on a story that the caller gives − such as, "I'm an old classmate of your husband's," or, "We were old army buddies." The next time the same caller telephones for your deceased husband, be ready with some pertinent questions which will convince you that the caller really did know your husband.

If you are single and a caller asks to speak to your husband, do not spout off and tell the caller that you are single, have never been married, and that you live alone. Ask the caller to identify himself and ask if you can take a message.

Sometimes people dial the wrong number and their errors may be reasonable. However, any time you receive a series of rude or wrong number telephone calls, report the incidents to the telephone company and the police department. If someone calls and asks, "Who is this?" or, "What number is this?" ask them to whom they wish to speak and what number they are calling. Never volunteer your telephone number, name, or address. If you are met with a steady stream of obscene language, hang up immediately without saying anything.

One of the most annoying crank callers is "the breather" type who calls you, says nothing, but breathes heavily into the telephone while you are saying hello, hello! Get ready for the crank by purchasing a shrill gymnasium whistle. The next time you answer the telephone and hear the breather, place the whistle in your mouth, cup your hands around the mouthpiece of the telephone and your mouth, then blow it long and hard. Another way to discourage the crank is to hold the telephone mouthpiece near a light switch and flip the switch on, or strike a metal ballpoint pen against the mouthpiece to imitate the sound of a tape recording machine being turned on. Pretend you are talking to someone else in the room, turn your head slightly away from the mouthpiece and say, "Well, you're the head supervisor of the telephone company, and this is the same caller − so do something about it. I told you this crank calls me every night!" Or say, "Yes, officer, this is the same caller again." Call the telephone company and ask to have your number changed, or request an unlisted number.

It takes about twenty minutes to trace a call. If you are really anxious to identify the crank, have the telephone company install an answering service that holds the caller on the phone and at the same time alerts the police to trace the call.

If you receive a call from a person posing as a salesman, insurance agent, or any other person who asks you to meet him in a restaurant, bar, park or any place, ask for his name, the name of the company he represents, and a number where you can call him back in a few minutes because you have some other business to attend to right away. Look up the name of the company or firm in your telephone directory, call the number in your directory, give them the name of the person who called you, and ask them if they employ such a person. If such a person is not employed by the company or there is no such company listed in your directory, 99% of the time the telephone number the caller gave will be phoney too. No matter how urgent or important the caller may make the conversation sound, take time to be certain the call is legitimate.

CALLING FOR HELP

While you are out emptying your trash, borrowing a cup of sugar, or picking up your mail from a downstairs mailbox, an intruder could enter your home or apartment. One of your best defenses would be to gain the privilege of using your telephone. It is possible that an intruder will allow you to make one telephone call if you can really make the call sound necessary and extremely urgent. For your call to be effective you must have previously selected a code message and have told two or three friends the code words and what to do if you ever call them and use those words. For example: "Have Everrett's Letter Posted (H E L P). I left it in my magazine on the hall table. He will really be worried if he does not hear from me." Or, "Please Let Elsie Help (P L E H, HELP backwards) you with the party tonight. I have a terrible headache and cannot come."

Some apartment buildings have an intercom system which operates the entrance door and requires the caller to lift up a telephone and press your apartment button. The person in the apartment deciding she wants the visitor to come in, presses a button located near the telephone, and it automatically unlocks the entrance door. Never press the button that releases the entrance door before you are sure who the caller is. Tell your visitors not to let any one else in the door at the same time you are letting them in.

If you want a telephone in your bedroom for protection, then have the telephone company install a second telephone, not an extension. Telephone extensions are designed for convenience, not necessarily for safety. A burglar who enters your home while you are in bed may spot your telephone in the living room and remove the telephone receiver from its cradle, or he may disconnect the wires by pulling them out of the wall, or cut them with a knife. In this case an extension would be inoperable, but a second phone could help you. Individuals who have two separate telephones list the most commonly used number in the telephone directory. The number for the second telephone should not be listed.

SUMMARY

Although the suggested telephone precautions are simple and undramatic, they should not be ignored. Personal protection, like property protection, is achieved through attention to seemingly unimportant details. The indiscreet revelation that you are a woman living alone can bring results that are neither simple nor undramatic. The telephone precautions are one effective means to avoid being victimized by a criminal.

Chapter Eight

TRAVEL PRECAUTIONS

INTRODUCTION

Travel for business and recreation is a part of the American way of life. The automobile has shaped our living, working and leisure habits into a drive-to, drive-in culture in which women are free to travel alone or without a male escort. For business and pleasure, by private car and public transportation, women today travel without hesitation — but not without danger to their personal safety. Illness, accidents, mechanical failures, wrong turns into dangerous or unfamiliar areas are potential situations which must be anticipated. To insure personal safety and to make the business or pleasure trip as enjoyable as possible, the following precautions should be heeded.

GENERAL PRECAUTIONS

1. Plan your trip and inform a trusted friend of your itinerary.
2. If you have a permanent disease or illness, carry a card in your wallet and wear a medi-alert bracelet explaining the type of condition you have.
3. Carry a first aid kit.
4. Know the name of your physician and his telephone number.
5. Know the name of your health insurance company and policy number.
6. If you are under 21 years of age, carry a letter of permission indicating that immediate medical attention may be given to you without consulting your parents or legal guardian. Be sure the letter is properly dated and signed by your parent or legal guardian.
7. Register in motels and hotels as M. Syperski, not Miss Mary Syperski or Mary Syperski.
8. Avoid striking up lengthy conversations with strangers.
9. Never invite strangers to your room.
10. Do not accept private tours, tours not conducted by employees of public agencies or resorts.
11. Never carry large amounts of cash. Keep large bills separated from smaller denominations. Avoid flashing large bills in public places.
12. Use travelers checks, but never carry all of them in one place, such as in your luggage. Make a list of the serial numbers from your travelers checks and carry this list some place other than in your purse.
13. Place name identification tags inside the lid and outside of luggage. Use your initials and last name only on all identification tags placed on the outside of luggage. If your luggage is a common make and color, tie a bright sash on the handle. This bright colored sash helps you to identify your luggage quickly, especially in airports where the luggage is simply piled in one area. The sash may prevent another individual who has similar type luggage from picking up your grip by mistake.

14. Credit card insurance policies are now available for short terms at low costs. Telephone your insurance agent and investigate the possibility of having your credit cards insured while you are on vacation.

CAR TRAVEL PRECAUTIONS

1. Have your automobile checked by a reputable mechanic to be certain that it is in top working condition and the tires are safe for the length of trip planned.
2. Avoid late night driving.
3. Never pick up hitchhikers.
4. Be sure your automobile insurance includes towing service.
5. Don't wait until the gasoline gauge indicates one-fourth full before you begin looking for a gas station. Plan your travel mileage so you will be certain to reach a sizeable town with a gasoline station.
6. Use well-traveled roads. Avoid shortcuts; they may be beautiful and sometimes shorter, but they are also usually deserted.
7. Keep your car doors locked at all times.
8. If you are traveling a long distance alone, arrange a couple of pillows with a coat and hat over them to make it look like someone is sleeping.
9. If you often drive alone at night, wear a man's hat to disguise your sex.
10. Never leave cameras and other valuables in public view on car seats when you have your automobile parked.
11. Use your trunk as much as possible; clothing hanging in the back seat is a dead give-away indicating you are traveling.
12. Never drive your convertible with the top down at night.
13. If lost, stop in a well-lighted, reputable nation-wide service station for directions.
14. Never take your road map into a restaurant to look over your route. This only draws attention to the fact that you are traveling.
15. Avoid traveling to "known" trouble areas to see what is going on.
16. Be extremely cautious when pulling off the road to sleep.
17. If camping, always stay in approved camping sites.

Car Trouble On The Road

1. Pull your car off the road.
2. Get out of your car and put the hood up; this will indicate you have car trouble.
3. Hang a handkerchief on the antenna or door handle.
4. Place a flare about 20 yards behind your car.
5. Get in your car, lock the doors and stay there until a police officer comes to your rescue.
6. Accepting a ride with a stranger is extremely dangerous. If strangers offer assistance, ask them if they would be so kind as to call a tow truck for you in the next town.
7. If for some reason you do accept a ride with a stranger to go for mechanical aid, write on a piece of paper the color, make, model, and license plate number of the car you intend to ride in and leave it in clear view inside your locked, dis-

abled car. Indicate on the note the time, date, and that you have gone for mechanical assistance with a stranger.

8. Never take off across fields, through woods, et cetera, on foot in search of help.
9. If you are on a service road that is adjacent to a main highway, try blinking your lights or honking your horn in an SOS fashion; a series of three short, three long, and three short flashes or honks.

PUBLIC TRANSPORTATION PRECAUTIONS

Stand in a well-lighted area, near the street if necessary, when waiting for a bus or taxicab. Never hide yourself in the shadows of a doorway or building on a dark street corner.

Stay close to the entrance or change-booth when waiting for an electric train, subway, or ferryboat. In many stations the waiting platform is a long way from the change-booth; a schedule planned in advance will help you determine when to leave the change-booth and walk swiftly to arrive at the platform at the same time your transportation does. Stay near the bow (front) of a ferryboat near the attendant and be ready to disembark immediately after the boat docks. Never loiter in the stern!

Trains are not always crowded; therefore, make every effort to get in a car that has at least a dozen occupants, or choose the car the motorman or conductor is in. If your car becomes sparsely populated, move to a car with more occupants. When riding on buses and trains, always sit in an aisle seat so you can move quickly if annoyed. Avoid the last seat or the inside seat, especially if it is late at night. If you are annoyed by another individual who is making improper advances or remarks, report it to the conductor or motorman immediately.

In most cities taxi drivers are safe to ride with alone, day or night. It is extremely rare for a woman to be approached or seduced by a taxi driver. Occasionally a gigolo will become a taxi driver, but he never lasts long because the other drivers soon become aware of his activities and report him, or one of his passengers reports him. This type of employee is fired immediately because no reputable cab company wants its reputation ruined.

SUMMARY

The purpose of travel precautions is the prevention and avoidance of situations which could endanger personal safety. But, because travel is so common, its dangers are easily ignored or forgotten until too late. The result is panic, which is in itself a further threat to personal safety. An awareness of, and preparation for, possible dangers can make travel safe and pleasurable. Now is the time to inaugurate the travel precautions set forth in this chapter; the best personal defense tactic is to avoid the necessity for personal defense.

Chapter Nine

RECREATION PRECAUTIONS

INTRODUCTION

Teenagers and young adults enjoy recreation away from the home and family. Free from family chaperones, they may drive or ride public transportation to where the action is. Beaches and parks, movie theaters, bowling alleys, bars, house parties, and lovers' lanes are popular recreation areas. Because these places are open to the general public and are unsupervised, dangerous situations can develop for a young woman who is alone. Therefore, (1) always have a male escort or female companion, (2) never provoke danger by your dress, speech, or action. These two rules should guide all of your public conduct.

BEACHES AND PARKS

Avoid going to the beach alone; plan to go with a friend. Never talk loudly or create a scene; your actions may attract the attention of undesirables. Do not flirt with strangers even though it may seem harmless. Use discretion in dressing. Your clothing or lack of clothing may attract the attention of a potential sex criminal. If an older man asks you to pose for snap shots, politely leave, take a swim, or visit with some friends nearby. Never go to a secluded part of the beach alone or only with another girl. Avoid talking with strangers; if a stranger asks you for the time and you have a watch, tell him the time and then look away, ignore him. Generally, this type of intruder will take the hint and move on. If he makes no effort to leave, ask him to please leave you alone. Few will continue to hang around. If one does, tell the lifeguard, brother, or anyone who might appear to be your brother, father, or a lifeguard.

Because any young group may attract a sex criminal, at picnics or special outings do not wander alone very far from the crowd or group you came with. In picnic areas or camp grounds never investigate old buildings that have been abandoned or closed up. These buildings may be unauthorized homes for bums or undesirables. Avoid old, unused trails in picnic areas, and do not go to undeveloped property in a park or camp site for your private meditation, particularly in areas where there is high grass, low bushes, and trees. Parks are desirable places for the sex criminal to attack a victim in seclusion.

MOVIES

If you are so foolish as to attend a movie unescorted, allow your eyes to become accustomed to the dark before taking a seat. Keep your purse on your lap or beside you in your own seat. If possible, sit next to a family or find a seat next to the aisle. From an aisle seat you can move quickly if annoyed by the masher type. Any incident in which an individual attempts to make improper advances toward you should be reported to the usher or manager. It is possible that you will solve your problem by moving to another seat; however, give a description of the annoying individual to an usher or theater manager who can keep a watchful eye on him so he does not succeed in trapping someone else who may not be able to move to another seat quickly.

Avoid sitting in dark corners or in the last rows of the balcony. These are frequent meeting sites for teenagers who can often find great pleasure in annoying unescorted women.

If someone really gives you trouble in a theater, and you are unable to handle the situation, let out a loud scream. If the attacker has a knife or gun and is using either to keep you still or get you to leave the theater with him, it is very unlikely he would actually use a weapon of this kind in a public place. A loud scream is the best defense because it will bring help immediately.

BOWLING ALLEYS

Bowling alleys should be used for bowling, not as hangouts or meeting places for the gang. Even sitting alone watching other people bowl may invite an annoying intruder. If you are bowling and discover you have attracted a spectator who is making loud remarks and crude comments or is trying to strike up a conversation with you, ignore him. Never accept food or drinks from a strange spectator; do not answer any of his questions, or indicate in any way that you have noticed his presence or comments. Press the button on your bowling station that summons the waitress and ask her to report the intruder to the manager.

If you have driven your car to a bowling alley or any other public place, park your car near the entrance, on a well-lighted street, or under a street light in a parking lot. Make sure you are not being followed when leaving any public place alone. Closely observe other persons that may be leaving the place at the same time you do. Any time you are on foot and are being followed, change your direction immediately, cross the street, stay on well-lighted busy streets, hail a cab, board a bus; get away!

BARS

A bar is an establishment whose main feature is the sale of liquor. If you go to a bar alone or with one or two other women, avoid sitting in a booth or at a table in a dark corner. Sit at the bar or a table in clear visual range of the bartender. Most bartenders will look after you or a party of all women approached or bothered by strangers. If a bartender or waitress serves you a drink upon the request of a stranger in the bar, do not accept the drink. Most respectable places have a policy which prohibits the waitress or bartender from serving drinks purchased by strangers. Do not divulge personal information — your name, the place where you live or work, your age, or telephone number — to any stranger in a bar or a cocktail lounge.

Nearly every bar, respectable or otherwise, has a few customers who are the type who give women the long look (up and down). Avoid having any kind of conversation with this type of individual. Ninety-five percent of the time, women who are annoyed by strangers in such establishments bring on the incidents themselves. Women often innocently encourage conversations with strangers because they are lonely, unhappy, single, have a miserable marriage, are new in town, have no friends, or simply want some male to talk with. Women who permit strangers picked up in a bar to escort them home are asking for trouble and are usually the same women who cannot understand how such a nice person could have attacked, assaulted, raped, or swindled them.

When annoyed by a persistent stranger, call the bartender as if you were going to order another drink; then quietly ask him for assistance. Be extremely cautious when leaving a bar if there has been an incident where the bartender or bouncer forced a stranger to leave the bar on your account. This individual may be mad enough to wait for you outside the bar. If there are several blocks between the bar and your car or public transportation, always call a taxi cab and ask the company dispatcher to have the driver come in for you. A two block ride in a cab may be better and cheaper than a two block walk into a death trap or assault.

PUBLIC BUILDINGS

Arenas

When attending a ball game, circus, carnival, dance, parade, or any other public function where there is sure to be a large crowd, anticipate that your pocketbook may be picked or stolen. Be sure you have a complete inventory of all credit cards with identification numbers, your driver's license number, and other pertinent information for all items you ordinarily carry in your purse. Keep your inventory of such items up-to-date and in a safe place where it can be found quickly if needed. Never carry your inventory sheet in your purse. If you do lose your purse or wallet, immediately advise the concerns where you have established credit card privileges to prevent your cards from being used by unauthorized persons.

Most forms of entertainment are interesting enough to divert your attention away from your purse or wrap. Carry a small purse with a handle, or a clutch bag near your body with one hand over the catch that opens the bag. Shoulder bags should be carried with the flap turned inward toward the body, preferably under the elbow; rest one hand over the flap that covers the opening at all times. Purses that have a long flexible strap for a handle can be carried safely by wrapping the strap once or twice around your wrist and grasping the clasp with your hand. Avoid carrying a large open type purse that is designed in the fashion of a short shopping bag. Things can be plucked from this type of bag with ease and speed even if it is deep.

Do not put cash in an envelope to carry in your purse, wallet, jacket pocket, or coat. The envelope can become lost or drop out of a coat pocket or purse easily. Since it is not the usual manner in which most people carry their money, envelopes containing money have been thrown away by forgetful individuals, or the jacket in which they kept an envelope containing money has been given away to the Salvation Army by a tidy spouse. The professional pickpocket can often check your pockets without your awareness of his hand, he moves so quickly. If you do catch him in the act of picking your pocket, grab his little finger or any finger and swiftly bend it back while you are screaming.

Elevators

Self-service elevators in lightly guarded buildings can be extremely dangerous. When using a self-service elevator, press the button for the floor you desire while you are still holding the door open. Do not allow the door to close until you see the arrow indicating your direction light up on the instrument panel. If the arrow points down and you want to go up, quickly step out of the elevator. Never ride the elevator down when you want to go up.

Do not step into an elevator carrying a lone, suspicious looking person; it will be worth your time to wait for the next elevator. Always stand near the instrument panel in an elevator; never step back in a corner if there is only one other person on board. If you are already on board an elevator, and the only other person in the elevator makes any improper advances, quickly place your hand over the emergency alarm button or reach for the emergency telephone.

Before taking an apartment in a large apartment building, ask some important questions concerning the elevator service: 1) Is it self-service? 2) Is a guard on duty at night? 3) If the trash cans, washing machines, or storage area is in the basement, does an intruder have access, or are tenants issued a key that must be used to open the elevator door that leads into the basement?

Rapes, assaults, and robberies do occur in elevators; yet most people, believing they will never be the victim of a criminal, fail to incorporate these simple rules into their daily life. These common sense tips on precaution and safety cannot possibly become habit unless you put them into practice each time you board an elevator regardless of the place and time of day or night.

Stores

Never leave your purse on a store counter while looking at the merchandise. A professional thief may be waiting for you to set your purse on a counter, on top of some of your packages, in a shopping bag, or on the floor. Remember the professional thief looks like anyone else and may be either male or female.

Under no circumstances should you leave your purse in a fitting or dressing room unattended for even a couple of minutes. Because purses are stolen or lost in dressing room facilities, warnings reminding you to take your purse with you are often posted.

When marketing do not put your purse in the shopping cart, especially if you leave the cart unattended while checking for an item in another aisle. Purses placed in the child's seat near the handle of the basket are especially handy for thieves. There was a rash of cases in which women reported their purses stolen in a large chain market. Two professional women thieves, dressed like shopping housewives, wheeled their cart beside the victim's cart. The victim was usually busy looking and picking out fruit or vegetables in the produce section of the store. One professional thief checked the aisle for other shoppers, and the other diverted the victim's attention by making a statement such as, "The lettuce really looks extra fresh and crisp today." The other professional snatched the victim's purse and hid it in her very large purse. In some instances a victim would get so involved in a conversation with one professional that her accomplice had time to check out her two or three items with the cashier, and was waiting outside in the car for her mate.

Restrooms

The female professional thief has found public restrooms in department stores, large restaurants, airports, and bus terminals ideally suited for stealing purses. Example: Mrs. X, using a public restroom in a large department store, hung her purse on the hook located on the inside of the cubicle door. In a few moments a hand reached over the top of the door and quickly snatched the purse free from the hook. By the time Mrs. X could pull herself together and get out of the cubicle, the thief was gone. She promptly reported the incident to the store manager who assured her they would telephone her at home if the purse was found.

The following morning about 10:00 a.m. Mrs. X received a telephone call from the department store stating that her purse had been found in a trash can and could be picked up on the 7th floor in room 741. She indicated that she would take a bus and could be in town about 11:30 a.m. When Mrs. X arrived at the store, she was unable to find room 741 on the 7th floor or any person who knew the whereabouts of her purse. The woman from the store who had telephoned Mrs. X had described her bag in detail, and Mrs. X was convinced the woman who telephoned her was in one of the offices in the store. She was still unable to locate her purse after shuffling back and forth between several offices. By 1:30 p.m. Mrs. X was confused and very disgruntled for having apparently made a trip to town for nothing.

You can probably guess what had happened in Mrs. X's absence. The thief who had stolen her bag had Mrs. X's money, her address, and the keys to her automobile and house. The thief, a member of a confidence gang, was th eperson who had telephoned her that morning. When she returned home that afternoon at 3:00 p.m., she found an empty house. All the furniture, curtains, wardrobe and linen closets were bare! Only the wall-to-wall carpets and the major built-in appliances in her kitchen remained. When the neighbors were questioned, it appeared that only one woman had noticed any activity around Mrs. X's house; a laundry truck had backed into the driveway. The neighbor did not know how long it had been there or when it left; she simply did not give it a second thought. She noticed the drapes were not on some of the front windows and assumed they were being sent out to be cleaned.

Mrs. X could have saved her property and a trip to town if she had been suspicious enough to call the manager of the department store and ask him to identify the caller as a legitimate employee.

PRIVATE PARTIES

Know your date! Avoid blind dates unless you are accompanied by another couple that you know well. Know where your date is taking you, and what time you expect to return home.

If you attend a party with a friend and discover the party is not the kind you had in mind, ask your date to take you home. If your date refuses, telephone your parents, brother, sister, or a close friend and ask to be picked up at the party. Under no circumstances should you leave the party unescorted and walk home or walk to public transportation. If you are unable to get a ride with someone you know, telephone for a taxi cab even though you have no money with you. When the taxi reaches home, ask the driver to wait while you go in and get the money.

Never be afraid to act the way you believe is right. Do not become annoyed or let it get you down if the crowd calls you a puritan, prude, or a square. Living with the standards you have set is sometimes very difficult; the results of lowering your standards may be even more difficult to live with.

LOVERS' LANE

Stay out of lovers' lanes or any isolated parking spot. It is natural for you to want to be alone with your date, but many secluded parking spots have become haunts for the sex criminal, too. One of the most common tricks of a sex criminal in lovers' lane is to locate a car that is parked away from any near-by cars. The criminal knocks on the window of the car if the door is locked and shines a very bright spotlight into the faces of the victims. The criminal then demands that the young man step out immediately. Blinded by the ultra bright light, the victim often takes it for granted that the individual with the flashlight is the police, and he opens the door unsuspecting. Or, if the door is not locked, the criminal swiftly opens the door, jerks the male out of the car and knocks him unconscious.

In one community young people would drive up a high hill that over-looked the city and park. Bill and Nancy were driving up the hill one night when Bill suddenly screeched to a halt as he came around a curve, for lying face down in the road was a man. Bill jumped from the car to give assistance. When Bill turned the man over, the man struck Bill in the head with a lug wrench. Nancy was raped and severely beaten. This particular incident happened several times to different couples before word got around that the dirt road was off limits because of the danger involved. Had Bill, Nancy, or their parents the courage to report the incident, it is very possible that the incidents which followed could have been prevented. When Bill saw the figure in the road, he should have backed up his car, turned around and headed for the nearest telephone for help.

SUMMARY

As with other personal and property safety precautions, the recreation precautions may appear to be very simple matters of common sense. Therefore, since everyone claims to have common sense, everyone is apt to nod agreeably, promptly forget all precautions, and continue to invite danger. Common sense will not make a credit card inventory sheet, common sense will not call a cab. Personal safety requires personal actions which demand immediate application of common sense knowledge. You must make the inventory sheet, you must call the cab, you must change the daily habits that threaten your safety.

Chapter Ten

CHILD SAFETY PRECAUTIONS

INTRODUCTION

The personal safety of children is the first and most serious responsibility of parenthood. In the act of procreation the parents not only create a life, but also a responsibility for the safety and well-being of that life. Failure to fulfill this obligation may result in serious injury to the child which a lifetime of regret and self-punishment will not undo. Because the child is an extension of the self, child defense is self-defense. Therefore, the child must be protected and taught to protect himself. Excluding accidents, molesters are the greatest threat to child safety. To train the child and to employ responsible baby sitters, parents should be aware of the characteristics and habits of child molesters.

CHILD MOLESTERS

Sex offenders are human products of our society who have made poor adjustments to fellow human beings and to the world perhaps because early relationships to parents, school, and community were inadequate. A sex molester is often erroneously thought of as an older man who waits in the dark and tries to lure a child into a deserted area. There is no typical profile of a molester. The offender looks like anybody else; however, normal sex relations make him anxious or afraid, so he avoids them. The molester is timid and generally undersexed rather than oversexed. Only half the problem is solved if these offenders are required to be sterilized because the sex drive persists.

Current knowledge concerning sex molesters indicates that in two out of three instances the victim has been previously acquainted with the offender.[67] The actual molesting takes place most frequently in the home of the offender or the victim, while theaters and automobiles rank third and fourth. Most acts are committed in the daytime. A large city found that 44% of reported acts occurred between 3:00 and 7:00 p.m. with lunch time being the next most prevalent time.[68]

In 1963 the state of Pennsylvania conducted a study to determine the ages of male offenders: five percent were over 50; three percent over 60; twenty percent between 16-20; nineteen percent between 21-25; and thirty-three percent between 26-40.[69] There is no available cure for the sex molester; however, with sufficient psychiatric treatment those who have a strong desire to change can often lead socially acceptable lives.

One authority sizes up potential victims as belonging in the following category:

"Most victims are from one to eight years of age; however, many cases involve boys and girls up to age sixteen. About one-sixth of the molested children resist and then rush to tell

[67]Beatrice Schapper, "What We Now Know About Sex Molesters", *Today's Health*, LXXXIX (January, 1966), pp. 18-19.

[68]*Ibid.*, pp. 19-21.

[69]*Loc. cit.*

their parents. The others passively accept, take part in, or even invite the incident. Some children who have an emotional lack in their homes return to the offender over a period of weeks or even years."[70]

The reaction of parents, relatives, friends, and others following an incident can be more disturbing to the victim than the actual attack. The amount of future psychological damage the child will have concerning sex depends on the attitude of those around him. The wise parent will keep calm and make every effort to help the child understand what happened and why. In this way the child feels accepted by his parents, and hopefully in a short time the whole affair will be forgotten.[71]

SAFETY RULES FOR CHILDREN

The following are eleven main points parents must explain and must be certain their child fully understand in order to help keep him safe from child molesters.

1. Never take a ride with a stranger in the family car or any strange car even if he tells you your parents want you, or that your brother asked him to give you a ride home.

2. Always take a friend with you if you are selling candy, cookies, magazine subscriptions, Christmas cards, or any other items.

3. Never play in or near public restrooms, in theaters, alleys, empty buildings, or any lonely or isolated places.

4. Never go to a movie theater alone. If anyone tries to touch you, get out of your seat immediately. Tell the usher or the man in charge of the theater. Never go with such a person to the bathroom or for a ride.

5. If a stranger asks you for directions, keep your distance; and under no circumstances should you enter the car.

6. Never accept candy, ice cream, or any other items from a stranger, no matter how friendly or insistent.

7. Never go into the house or room of a stranger or casual acquaintance even if he tells you that he has something pretty or nice to give or show you.

8. If someone does try to get you or your playmate into a strange automobile, write down the license number by scratching it on the ground with a stick if you do not have a pencil or paper. Tell your parents and the police immediately.

9. Never take shortcuts that go through alleys, long dark streets, or empty lots where trees, low bushes, or tall grass are growing.

10. Never allow anyone, including friends or relatives, to touch or fondle intimate parts of your body. If someone tries to caress your body, whether you know them or not run as quickly as you can and inform your parents and the police.

11. Never let acquaintances into the house when you are alone.

Failure to learn or observe these rules may result in unexpected disaster as the following example illustrates:

[70]*Ibid.*, pp. 78-81.
[71]*Ibid.*, pp. 80-81.

One day an eleven year old girl did not feel well. Since both parents worked, she stayed home from school alone. The mother telephoned the girl at ten in the morning and again at noon to check on her. When the father returned home at three-thirty in the afternoon, he found his daughter dead and wrapped only in a bed sheet. The girl had been molested and stabbed. The police found finger prints on a glass and other clues that led to the arrest and conviction of a neighbor man known to both the girl and the parents. The accused testified that he only wanted someone to talk with, had seen the girl through a dining room window, and decided he would visit with her. He rang the door bell and the girl invited him in. They both drank some iced tea; then the accused could not remember exactly what had happened.

An innocent child trusts — but not always wisely. Therefore, parents can never take for granted the child's safety. The parents must teach their children the safety precautions and must stress the significance of always obeying them exactly.

Most children twelve and under are not old enough to assume the responsibility of babysitting or staying alone. Yet, it is true that some parents will leave a nine or ten year old home alone for a few hours in the evening. This practice can be extremely dangerous, especially if the parents have neglected to inform the child of specific ways to protect himself and what to do in case of an emergency. For example, teaching a child a simple thing like dialing "O" for the telephone operator for help could very well save a life. Parents must teach their children how to protect themselves without making the child fearful of all strangers.

For self-protection, instruct children to keep all the doors and windows locked. Under ordinary circumstances children should be told not to open a door to callers. If the parents expect a caller, they should give a brief description of their friend and tell each child the approximate time of his arrival. Show each child how to look outside and view a caller without being seen.

Parents should leave the telephone number where they can be reached, or a relative's phone number to call in case of an emergency. By the time a child is 6 years old, he should know the procedure for reporting emergencies to the police. These numbers, along with the local police department number, should be left on a pad of paper or in a designated book beside the telephone. A pencil for writing messages should be readily handy. If the telephone rings and a child is home alone, he should never indicate to a strange voice that he is alone. A child should tell the caller that the person he wants to speak with is busy right now but will return the call shortly if he wishes to leave his name and telephone number.

If an intruder succeeds in entering the home, the child should seek aid by leaving the house by another door or by calling for help through a window. Children can learn to pick out significant characteristics of an individual if the parents stage a few practice sessions. When confronted by an intruder, the child should notice clothing, rings, scars, distinguishing features, tatoos, voice quality, and physical characteristics.

It is unfortunate that in our society a child must take such precautions for his own safety. Yet the dangers exist, and the parent who fails to protect and train his child increases the possibility of those dangers becoming realities.

BABYSITTING

The employer is responsible for selecting a sitter who is competent to protect the children; and the sitter, accepting the job, assumes the parental duties of safeguarding the children. The babysitter should observe the following precautions:

Never leave the children unattended. Do not allow your friends in the house unless you have obtained prior permission from your employer. Never allow strangers into the house. Learn the physical set-up of the house. Know where all exterior doors are located and check them to be certain they are locked. Know where the telephone and extensions are located. Know where the employer can be reached in case of emergency. Look for a weapon you might use to protect yourself should you ever be confronted with an intruder. Protective weapons might be such items as a candlestick holder, fireplace poker, golf club, or bottle.

Know where the children should store their yard toys when they finish playing with them. Toys that are not put away are considered an attractive nuisance. Don't make it easy for a thief by leaving bicycles, wagons, or other toys in the street, on the lawn, porch, or driveway.

If you have difficulty controlling the children, never threaten to call the police if they fail to behave immediately. Do not spank or strike the children unless you have written permission from your employer; you could be charged with assault and battery.

SUMMARY

Child safety precautions are necessary. The parent has the responsibility of establishing the difficult balance between over-protectiveness and inadequate protection. The child must be neither watched over continually nor be abandoned to his own resources. The parent must train the child in protective precautions. The training, given properly, will not only protect the child from molesters and other dangers, but will also aid him in the maturing process. The training should not instill fear in the child, but a sense of pride in knowing how to take care of himself. A baby-sitter should take as careful precautions with children as do their parents.

PART IV

WEAPONS AND TECHNIQUES
OF
PERSONAL DEFENSE

Chapter Eleven

WEAPONS

INTRODUCTION

Personal and property safety are the results of taking precautions and personal defense measures. The precautions, discussed in the preceding chapters, are methods of protecting person and property by deterring and avoiding the criminal. Personal defense is the method of protecting yourself and property when physically encountering a criminal. Despite all precautions such a confrontation may occur, and therefore learning the weapons and techniques of personal defense is important in order to help counteract a criminal's attack.

The primary objective of personal defense is escape; the secondary objective is apprehension of the criminal by the proper authorities. These objectives determine your choice of weapons and techniques for self-defense. A weapon or technique that fulfills both objectives is one that temporarily incapacitates and also marks the criminal for possible later identification. However, a weapon or technique that permanently injures or kills an attacker creates the possibility of legal liability; and a weapon or technique that does not effect your escape may result in your death. Thus, the stakes are high; success will require great mental and physical effort, training and practice. The remainder of the book advises you of your legal rights of self-defense, and the legality of weapons; teaches you weapon skills, body conditioning, and counterattack skills and techniques.

THE RIGHT OF SELF-DEFENSE

Laws pertaining to the citizen's rights of self-defense are changing. You should know the laws of your state and be aware of the fact that: "He who acts in self-defense does so at his own peril; his act must be that of the ordinary, careful, and prudent individual, and the jury is the judge of the reasonableness of his conduct."[72]

There are, though, a number of situations recognized by law in which the use of force, even deadly force, may be excused or justified. In New York[73] and California deadly force may be employed whenever one reasonably believes that he may receive serious bodily injury by another, or is placed in imminent peril of death, or believes that the killing of the other is necessary to save his own life.[74]

Justifiable homicide exists only when the killing is actually or apparently necessary.[75] For example, if a trespasser is threatening no felonious attempt, the act is not sufficient to warrant the owner to make use of a deadly weapon in order to repel the trespasser. The right of self-defense exists only as long as the threatened danger continues to exist. If a threatened victim shoots the attacker who falls to the ground and so is

[72]Charles W. Fricke, *California Criminal Law* (Los Angeles, California, Legal Book Store, 1961), p. 172.

[73]Weinberger, *op. cit.*, Part II, p. 5, column 1-2.

[74]*Penal Code of the State of California, 1966 Supplement* (Dearing, Bancroft-Whitney Company, 1966), Article 197.

[75]*Loc. cit.*

incapable of inflicting bodily injury, then danger no longer exists; if thereafter the victim fires a fatal shot, he is considered guilty of homicide regardless of the fact that the first shot was justified under the law of self-defense.

Fear of great bodily injury to himself alone does not justify a victim to kill an attacker. The situation and circumstances must be such that any reasonable and prudent person placed in the same situation would believe the danger of serious bodily injury to be present. The rest of this chapter discusses the legality of weapons.

GUNS

The Second Amendment to the United States Constitution grants citizens the right to bear arms. This right carries with it the responsibility to know the legal uses and the proper care of weapons. Guns are probably the most effective personal defense weapon; but because they are also legally and physically the most dangerous, the possession and use of guns is not recommended for personal defense. In the absence of any federal gun control laws, the individual cities, counties, and states have passed regulatory legislation, most of which is a lawyer's nightmare. The following discussion on concealed weapons is only one example of the confusion and contradictions in existing laws and their interpretation in our country.

Concealment is an essential element of the federal offense of carrying a weapon.[76] One is said to have a concealed weapon if it is on his person or if it is carried in his clothing. "A weapon is carried on or about the person in violation of statute when it is carried in such proximity to the person as to be convenient of access within immediate physical reach, as when it is in the hand, or in clothing worn or carried by the accused." [77]

According to the interpretation of some authorities, when a weapon is merely in a vehicle in which the accused is riding, and when the weapon is not attached to his person, it cannot be said to be carried on or about the person.[78] But in other cases the court refused to recognize this rule where the weapon was on[79] or under[80] the seat of the vehicle, or was accessible, even though not on or under the seat.[81]

In some jurisdictions, however, or under certain circumstances a different rule prevails; it contends that a weapon was not carried on or about the person when it was under the seat[82] or on the floor of an automobile,[83] or in a pocket of the door,[84] or in a dashboard compartment.[85] Where a local or state statute requires concealment as an element of the offense, it is no offense to carry a weapon in a vehicle if the weapon is not concealed.[86]

Other laws also seem irrational; the fact that a weapon may not be lawfully bought or sold in a city does not mean that it is illegal to own a weapon in that city; the weapon may be purchased in another city or by mail order.

[76]Francis J. Ludes, Harold J. Gilbert, et al editorial staff, *Corpus Juris Secundum,* A complete restatement of the entire American law, XCIV (New York, American Law Book Company, 1956), p. 481, Illinois—People v. Liss.

[77]*Ibid.*, p. 492.

[78]*Ibid.*, p. 493, Tex. – Hardy v. State.

[79]*Loc. cit.*, Tex. – Garrett v. State.

[80]*Loc. cit.*, Tex. – Emerson v. State.

[81]*Loc. cit.*, Tex. – DeFriend v. State.

[82]*Loc. cit.*, Florida – Watson v. Stone.

[83]*Loc. cit.*

[84]*Loc. cit.*

[85]*Loc. cit.*, Ky. – Elza v. Commonwealth.

[86]*Ibid.*, p. 494, Cal. – People v. Commons.

A person using a firearm or other weapon in self-defense is not liable for injury unintentionally inflicted upon a bystander unless he is guilty of negligence or folly in the use of the weapon. [87] So long as he acts as a reasonably prudent man would act in a similar situation, he is not liable.[88] Thus, when a person in lawful self-defense shoots at an assailant, and, missing him, accidently wounds an innocent by-stander, he is not liable for the injury if guilty of no negligence.[89] However, proving no negligence may not be easy in a court of law.

In addition to these legal liabilities, guns are also physically dangerous for the owner and his family. The owner of a gun must assume the responsibility of cleaning, oiling, and caring for the weapon so that it will operate properly when needed. Many persons purchase guns for protection, but do not know how to use them. The only way to learn gun safety and shooting accuracy is by taking lessons at a shooting club or range. No dwelling is safe with a loaded gun on the premises even if it is hidden on the top shelf of a closet or cupboard or in the back of a bureau drawer; for there is simply no safe place for a loaded gun. Children far too often manage to gain access to these weapons. Gun accidents in the home account for many needless deaths of children as well as adults every year in this country. Then, too, if the owner cannot load the gun in the dark or when blindfolded, the individual has no business owning such a weapon for personal defense. Because of the legal and physical dangers, guns are not recommended personal defense weapons.

ILLEGAL WEAPONS

The carrying or possession of a particular weapon is unlawful when, and only when, such weapons are prohibited by state statute; that is, the weapon must come within the meaning of the terms employed in the statutes designating forbidden weapons.[90] In this connection the courts have construed the meaning of such general designations as "arms,"[91] "firearms,"[92] "Instruments,"[93] "contraband,"[94] or "weapons" generally. [95] Also, the lawmaking body frequently designates by names the weapons or instrument which may not be possessed because they are notoriously used for criminal purposes. Possession of any of the following weapons may be illegal, irrespective of any intent to use the weapon unlawfully: billies,[96] blackjacks, [97] bludgeons,[98] bowie knives,[99] brass knuckles, [100] metal knuckles, [101] saps,[102] dirks, [103] dangerous knives,[104] daggers, [105]

[87]Edwin Stacey Oakes, George S. Gulick et al editorial staff, *American Jurisprudence,* LVI (New York, The Lawyers Co-operative Publishing Company, 1947), p. 1009, Okla. – Shaw v. Lord.

[88]*Loc. cit.*

[89]*Loc. cit.*

[90]Ludes and Gilbert, *op. cit.,* p. 487, Cal. – People v. Golden.

[91]*Loc. cit.,* Puerto Rico – People v. Vadi.

[92]*Loc. cit.,* U.S. – U.S. v. Freeman.

[93]*Loc. cit.,* Puerto Rico – People v. Acevedo.

[94]*Loc. cit.,* U.S. – U.S. v. One 1950 Pontiac Convertible Coupe.

[95]*Loc. cit.,* Iowa – State v. Williams.

[96]*Loc. cit.,* Cal. – People v. Canales.

[97]*Loc. cit.*

[98]*Loc. cit.,* N.Y. – People v. Visarities.

[99]*Loc. cit.,* Tex. – Brito v. State.

[100]*Loc. cit.,* Cal. – People v. Quinones.

[101]*Ibid.,* p. 476, Ky. – Perry v. Commonwealth.

[102]*Loc. cit.,* Cal. – People v. Rogers.

[103]*Ibid.,* p. 487, Cal. – People v. Ruiz.

[104]*Loc. cit.,* N.Y. – People v. Cricuoli.

[105]*Loc. cit.,* Tex. – Bivens v. State.

razors,[106] slung shots,[107] concealable pistols or revolvers,[108] and other particular instruments, including machine guns,[109] and sawed-off shotguns.[110] Furthermore, a deadly weapon does not cease to be such by becoming temporarily inefficient, nor is its essential character changed by disassembling it if the parts may be easily re-assembled to be effective again.

LEGAL HAND WEAPONS

Most states legalize the use of the following objects or weapons for defense against an attacker:

1. Long, five-cell flashlight.

2. Rolled up magazine or newspaper — roll a magazine the size of "Life" or "Post", or a 25-30 page section of any newspaper rolled tightly. Fasten the magazine or newspaper with three or four rubber bands, or tie it with string so it will stay tightly rolled.

3. Umbrella.

4. Finger nail file — with a good handle so you can grip it securely.

5. Stiff hair brush or steel comb.

6. Hard bound book — consisting of 250-300 pages.

7. Purse.

8. High heels or wedge shoes.

9. Keys.

10. Hairspray.

A few states permit the use of other weapons for self-defense: (Check the Penal Code of your state.)

1. Hat pins.

2. Shock rods—often used by police to control people in a riot area. It is approximately twelve inches long and can be carried in a pocket or handbag. The rod operates with regular flashlight batteries which supply sufficient current to be converted by a transistorized circuit into a 4,000 volt charge. The charge is safe but yet powerful enough to temporarily incapacitate the largest assailant.

3. Tear gas — General's MK II Pocket Tear Gas Protector, and General's MK IV Chemical Mace fire a pattern of tear gas droplets. Only the face which comes in contact with the droplets is affected; consequently, other persons in the same room or area are not bothered by the discharge. Both the MK II and IV will subdue the attacker completely without permanent injury.

4. Spray-Gard — stops aggressors. It comes in a plastic bottle that fits in a woman's purse easily. Spray-Gard causes agonizing pain and will incapacitate an attacker for a half-hour or more; yet it is safe, legal, unlike tear gas or guns. Spray-Gard stains the attacker — aiding the police in identifying the assailant.

[106]*Loc. cit.*, W. Va. — Claiborne v. Chesapeake and O. Ry. Company.
[107]*Loc. cit.*, Tex. — Vargas v. State.
[108]*Loc. cit.*, N.Y. — People v. Woods.
[109]*Ibid.*, p. 488.
[110]*Loc. cit.*

Individual cities and states have different laws regarding the possession and handling of self-defense weapons as well as guns. Before choosing a hand weapon, check the local and state laws. A weapon is effective only if it is legal and if you know how to use it. The next chapter teaches the effective use of weapons.

SUMMARY

When your person or property is threatened by direct encounter with a criminal, defense weapons and techniques can protect you from injury or death. The proper choice and use of hand weapons for counterattack is very important. Although the United States Constitution grants the right to bear arms, a gun is not a recommended weapon except for gun experts. Individual cities and states have different laws regarding weapons and self-defense. Before choosing a hand weapon, check the legal regulations in your state's Penal Code. The purpose of personal defense is escape; therefore, the weapons should temporarily incapacitate, not permanently injure or kill. The hand weapons recommended in this chapter are legal and effective deterrents against attack.

Chapter Twelve

WEAPON SKILLS

INTRODUCTION

An effective weapon of self-defense is not an object, but the skillful use of an object. The object — weapon — may be a hand weapon such as a nail file, purse, umbrella; or it may be a personal weapon such as your hand, knee, foot, or voice. None of these weapons are endowed with a magic to ward off the attacker and permit your escape. On the contrary, if the hand weapons are not used properly, they can be seized by the attacker and used against you. Therefore, it is extremely important that you learn your weapon skills very well.

A successful counterattack is based on surprise, focus, and follow-through. Because you lack the strength of a male, your defense must come as a surprise which catches an attacker off guard. Your counterattack must be focused on a vulnerable part of the assailant's body in order to temporarily incapacitate him and enable you to escape.

VULNERABLE TARGETS OF THE HUMAN BODY

The human body has numerous structural weaknesses which are definitely vulnerable targets to attack. Unconsciousness, severe pain, or even death may be caused by applying pressure or delivering blows to these major, vulnerable targets. Learn their locations (see Figures 11, 12, and 13).

ANTERIOR VIEW

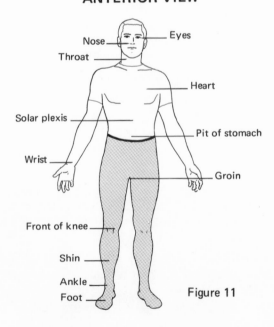

Figure 11

LATERAL VIEW

POSTERIOR VIEW

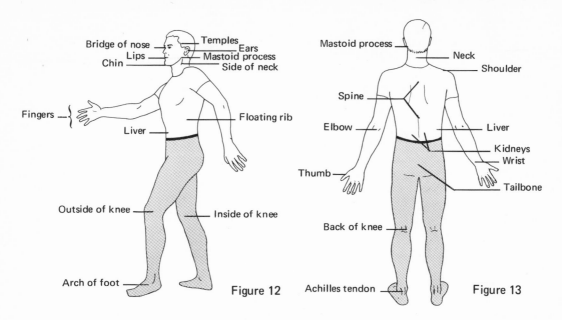

Figure 12

Figure 13

HAND WEAPON SKILLS

Since the vulnerable parts of the body are effective targets, you must take advantage of them when defending yourself with a hand weapon. If you choose to use a hand weapon, it is extremely vital that you develop a high degree of proficiency with it so that it will not be seized and used against you. There are many hand weapon skills to learn well, the application of each depending on the weapon you use:

1. Long, five cell flashlight — use in a jabbing manner to the face or stomach, or strike the inside or outside of the knees or ankles.

2. Rolled up magazine or newspaper — use in a ramming fashion into the abdominal area or face, particularly directly under the nose or into the throat.

3. Umbrella — place one hand near the center of the umbrella and the other hand slightly behind it; use in a quick jabbing fashion to the abdominal area.

4. Finger nail file — carry it in your hand or in your purse as the situation requires. Use it in a jabbing fashion with a quick upward thrust.

5. Stiff hair brush or steel comb — use in a slashing or raking motion across the face or tendons on the back of the attacker's hand.

6. Hard bound book — hold with both hands and smash its flat surface into the face of the attacker, or hold with one hand and strike the bound edge of the book into the side of the neck or throat. A BIG wind-up will give the attacker time to get into a position to block your blow and possibly grab the book away from you.

7. Purse — hold in both hands and use it in a pushing manner toward the face. Do not swing the purse at the assailant because it can easily be grabbed out of your hand; it gives the attacker time to duck, and your chances of losing your balance are great.

8.   High heels or wedge shoes — use a heel grind into the arch of the attacker's foot, or remove your shoe and strike the attacker around the head and neck area.

9.   Keys — with keys sticking out between the fingers (see Figure 14A and 14B). Use a fist blow to the face and neck, or scrape the keys across the tendons of the attacker's hand.

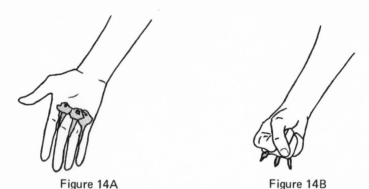

Figure 14A   Figure 14B

10.   Hairspray — direct the spray to the attacker's eyes and face. Never strike a match to the stream of spray converting the can into a flame thrower. Many people have been severely burned and the chance of the can blowing up is great.

11.   Hat pin — carry it in a handy place in your handbag or carry it in your hand if you cannot avoid walking in a dangerous area. If you are required to use a hat pin, hold it securely in the hand and use it in a quick upward jabbing motion.

12.   Shock rod — carry it in the hand when walking alone on dark streets. To use it against an attacker, merely touch the rod to the skin of his hands, wrist, neck or face.

13.   Tear gas — aim the stream of tear gas droplets toward the attacker's face. Your aim depends on your distance from the attacker and whether or not you are in a high wind. Gravity pulls the droplets downward; consequently, you will need to aim slightly above the attacker's head in order for the droplets to strike his face and be effective.

14.   Spray-Gard — squeeze the bottle firmly aiming at the attacker's face. The spray is fine spray similar to hair spray. The effectiveness of this hand weapon decreases as the distance between you and the attacker increases.

PERSONAL WEAPON SKILLS

Personal weapons are the parts of your body you can use for self-defense when you have no other items to convert into a reliable weapon. Developing the ability to use your personal weapons efficiently and effectively will take practice. Although personal weapons can be used successfully to incapacitate an assailant, they become increasingly important and more effective when used in conjunction with personal defense techniques as described in chapter fourteen.

HEAD BUTTING

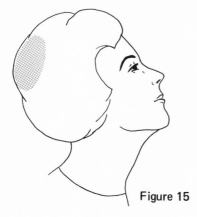

Figure 15

POSITION OR ACTION	TARGETS
Bend knees	Mouth
Clinch teeth	Chin
Keep mouth firmly shut	Nose
	Lips
	Pit of stomach

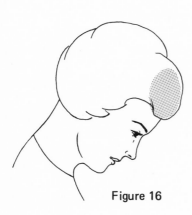

Figure 16

HEEL OF HAND

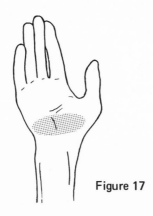

Figure 17

POSITION OR ACTION	TARGETS
Slightly spread fingers apart	Chin
Bend wrist	Nose
Deliver blow upward	Wrist

EDGE OF HAND BLOW

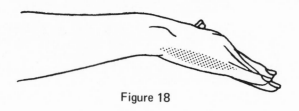

Figure 18

POSITION OR ACTION	TARGETS
Wrist straight and firm	Bridge of nose
Palm down	Lips
chop across the body, or	Throat
Palm inward	Spine
chop in a downward motion	Kidneys
	Side or back
	of neck

CUPPED HAND BLOW

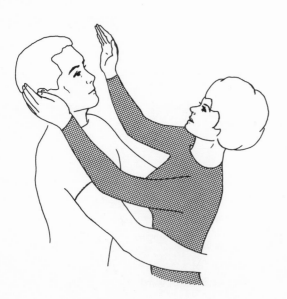

POSITION OR ACTION	TARGETS
Wrists straight and firm	Ears
Elbows slightly flexed,	
but firm	
Slightly cup hands	

Figure 19

EDGE OF FIST BLOW

Figure 20

POSITION OR ACTION

Wrist straight and firm

Keep distal joint of bent thumb pressed firmly across middle digit of first finger

Bend knees

Power comes from elbow, shoulder, and legs

TARGETS

Bridge of nose

Lips

Liver

Groin

Side or back of neck

Throat

Floating ribs

Spine

Kidneys

FIST BLOW

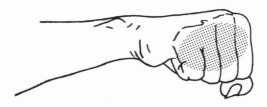

Figure 21

POSITION OR ACTION

Wrist straight and firm

Keep bent thumb pressed firmly across middle digits of first two fingers

Bend knees

Power comes from elbow, shoulder, and legs

TARGETS

Chin

Mastoid process

Heart

Solar plexus

Pit of stomach

FOREARM BLOW

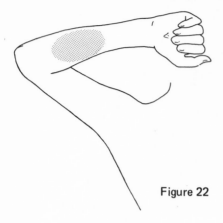

POSITION OR ACTION   *TARGETS*
Elbow fully flexed   Face
Hold arm shoulder-high   Ears
Swing arm forward and
  toward the inside

Figure 22

ELBOW BLOW

Figure 23

POSITION OR ACTION   *TARGETS*
Keep elbow fully flexed   Eyes
Move elbow directly back-   Nose
  ward or outward across   Mouth
  the body   Chin
    Pit of stomach

EXTENDED KNUCKLE BLOW

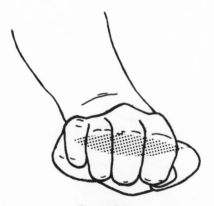

POSITION OR ACTION   *TARGETS*
Bend fingers firm and   Temples
  rigid   Throat
Wrist straight and firm
Bend knees
Power comes from elbow,
  shoulder, and legs

Figure 24

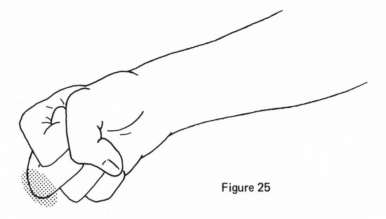

Figure 25

Fig. 25	*POSITION OR ACTION*	*TARGETS*
KNUCKLE DIG	Wrist and fingers firm	Tendons on
	Force the knuckle of the second finger to protrude	back of hand
	Rotate knuckles in a grinding fashion	
HAND PRESSURE	Slightly cup hand	Under nose
	Slightly spread fingers	Throat
	Bend wrist	
	Cover target with palm of hand and press firmly	
THUMB PRESSURE	Wrist firm	Mastoid process
	Place hand around attacker's throat	
	Press thumb firmly against target directly under ear	
THUMB GOUGE	Wrist and thumb firm	Eyes
FINGER JAB	Fingers rigid	Eyes
PINCH AND TWIST	Wrist firm	Lips
	Grab fleshy part and twist	Ears
FINGERNAIL SCRATCH	Slightly cup hand	Face
	Fingers bent and rigid	Throat
	Claw and scratch vigorously in a short raking manner	Neck
		Hands
BITING	Hold jaw firm	Ears
	Neck straight and rigid	Lips
		Neck
		Arms

HAIR PULLING	Grab small amount of hair Twist and pull	Head Chest
COUNTER JOINT MOVEMENTS	Bend twist or turn the limb Force joint to move in opposite direction from its normal function	Wrist Fingers Thumb Elbow Shoulder Knee Ankle Foot

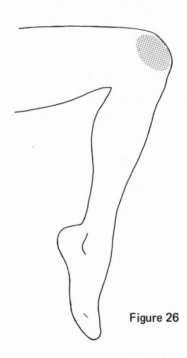

Figure 26

	POSITION OR ACTION	*TARGETS*
Fig. 26 KNEE LIFT	Fully flex knee After using, immediately return foot to floor to maintain balance	Face Chin Floating ribs Liver Groin
KNEE DROP	Full flex knee Immediately recover to your feet and run for help	Chest Solar plexus Pit of stomach Kidneys Spine

 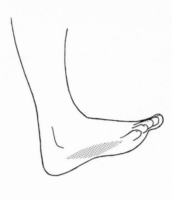 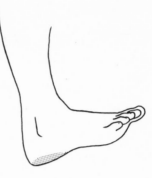

Figure 27   Figure 28   Figure 29

	POSITION OR ACTION	TARGETS
Fig. 27 kick with toes and ball of foot	When kicking forward, kick with toes and ball of foot Keep the knee of the leg you are not kicking bent Immediately lower kicking foot to floor and run for help	Temples Heart Floating ribs Liver Solar plexus Pit of stomach Kidneys Groin Spine Tailbone Back, front, inside, or outside of knees

	POSITION OR ACTION	TARGETS
Fig. 28 KICK SIDEWARD	When kicking sideward kick with edge of foot Immediately return kicking foot to floor to maintain balance	Temples Floating ribs Liver Outside of knee Shins

	POSITION OR ACTION	TARGETS
Fig. 29 HEEL GRIND	Flex knee Stamp and grind heel in a twisting fashion	Arch of foot

SUMMARY

Weapon skills are the basis of successful personal defense. The vulnerable parts of the body must be learned, and counterattacks must be studied and practiced. Only through practice will you acquire the confidence that is necessary to surprise and incapacitate your assailant. The following discussion will demonstrate some suggested procedures for using your weapon skills.

If you are assaulted, keep your wits alert. Scream as loudly as possible. Run! Try to get away; then immediately call the police and give an accurate description of the assailant and any other details involved in the incident. Even a mediocre description can often help the police locate and arrest your would-be attacker. You may have had time to notice scars; tattoos; type and color of clothing (suit, work clothes, hat or hatless); color of hair; approximate height, weight, age; color, make, model, and license of automobile if one is involved.

If you are hastily running away from an assailant and suddenly realize you are going to be overtaken, quickly turn and face the attacker. Immediately try to determine the attacker's capability, motive, and state of mind. The moment you face your attacker you must make up your mind as to your course of action. If you feel you are simply unable to put up a fight, let the marauder have your purse; perhaps this will satisfy him. If you decide to defend yourself, put every ounce of strength you have into the defensive tactic or tactics you feel most competent in executing. The assailant does not expect you to resist in any way. The decision to defend yourself can be one advantage in your favor because of the element of SURPRISE involved. The sole purpose of your defense is to incapacitate the attacker momentarily, allowing yourself the opportunity to run and get away. In this regard strike the temples, bridge of nose, throat, or side of neck with a book or purse. Use an umbrella, rolled up newspaper or magazine in a ramming fashion into the solar plexus, "bread basket", or under the nose.

When without a book, purse, or other items to convert into defensive weapons, use your own personal weapons. Place the heel of your hand under the attacker's nose and apply pressure, or use a swift blow with the heel of your hand under his nose. Either action will cause immediate, copious bleeding to momentarily disable your attacker. Pinch the attacker's lips with your fingers and twist vigorously. Bite his ears, fingers, hands, or arms. Use the edge of the hand blow; holding your wrist straight with your hand held stiff and firm, chop the bridge of the assailant's nose, Adam's apple, temple, or the side of his neck. Scratch his face and throat with your fingernails. With all your strength swiftly thrust your knee into his groin.

If attacked from the rear, grasp the attacker's little finger firmly (use both of your hands) and vigorously pull it back. This defensive tactic can break the little finger, or at least dislocate it. Step firmly down on the top of the instep or arch of the assailant's foot; press all of your weight onto your heel and grind your heel into this vulnerable point. Butt the back of your head sharply into the aggressor's face particularly against the lips, nose, chin, or ears. Kick the heel of your shoe directly into the shin or scrape the heel of your shoe up and down against the shin. Dig your knuckles into the tendons on the back of the assailant's hands.

Never try to beat the assailant to a pulp. Defend yourself, temporarily incapacitate the attacker, then quickly get away. Never try to run with high heeled shoes on. Telephone the police as soon as possible.

If you are on foot and realize you are being followed, try to get away. Make a dash for the porch of the first house that has lights on inside. By all means SCREAM and try to attract attention. When downtown, try to hail a cab or board a bus. If a car should follow you, change direction and run toward a busy street. Your change of direction forces the car to make a U-turn or go around the block in order to continue following.

Never carry illegal weapons such as guns, knives, or billy clubs. The attacker can grab the weapon away, and you may become the victim of your own weapon. Also, if you were to injure someone with an illegal weapon, you would be liable and could be sued or jailed.

Obviously you would not be able to use all of the skills suggested above at one time. Choose at least two hand weapon skills and six personal weapon skills to practice against an imaginary opponent. For example, practice the edge of the hand blow by striking a table top, or practice jabbing by thrusting a rolled up newspaper into a throw rug placed over a clothes line. Practice until you feel confident in using these skills to defend yourself.

Chapter Thirteen

BODY CONDITIONING
FOR PERSONAL
DEFENSE TECHNIQUES

INTRODUCTION

In addition to the weapon skills, personal defense includes throws and counter movements. These techniques, fully discussed and illustrated in the next chapter, cannot be executed safely by an inflexible or weak body. If muscles are tight from insufficient activity, they may be easily strained or pulled by sudden movements; and although the principle of leverage is used extensively in defense techniques, muscular strength is necessary. Rolls and falls, which are basic movements of defense techniques, must also be practiced. Body conditioning exercises, which develop flexibility, strength, and endurance, prepare your body for personal defense and firm and tone your muscles for a more attractive personal appearance.

Flexibility is the range of motion you have at a specific joint. The range of motion is determined by the ability of the involved antagonist muscles to stretch. Flexibility exercises are necessary to stretch the muscles. However, individuals vary in muscle structure; consequently, individuals will achieve varying degrees of success in doing the exercises.

Strength exercises to maintain controlled action at joints should always accompany flexibility exercises. Strength exercises involve slow, sustained movements and the use of weighted objects and resistance. Muscular strength is essential in holding body segments in good alignment while sitting, standing, or moving. Emergency movements needed in personal defense techniques require more strength than ordinary activities. It is important for every woman to have some reserve strength at her command.

Before the personal defense techniques can be practiced, the body must be conditioned. If the body is insufficiently "warmed-up", the muscles can be easily pulled, strained, or cramped by the stress of the vigorous personal defense movements. When executed properly, the flexibility and strength exercises provide a total body "work out" which increases respiration and pulse rates so that the working muscles receive the oxygen necessary for efficient motion.

Select at least three flexibility and three strength exercises which require the use of as many different body areas as possible. Repeat each exercise ten times; as you increase your strength and flexibility, increase your repetitions until you are able to do three sets of ten repetitions with a one minute rest period between each set of ten. For variety you may change your selection of exercises from time to time.

FLEXIBILITY EXERCISES

Purpose: Increase flexibility of the back.

Starting
Position: Sit on floor with soles of feet together and grasp ankles with your hands
                (see Fig. 30 A).

Action: Slowly pull your trunk forward, lowering your head toward your feet (see
                Fig. 30 B).

                NOTE: Do not bounce! Pull–, lower–, hold–, and slowly return to the
                starting position with trunk erect (see Fig. 30A).

                To stretch the adductors while resting in the starting position, press down-
                ward on the knees with your hands as you pull up against the ankles.

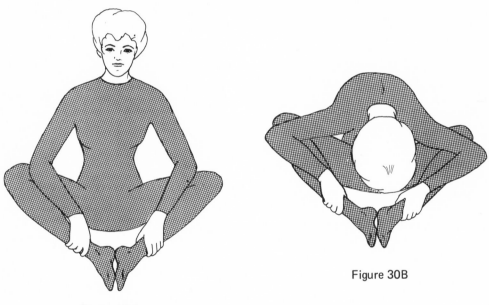

Figure 30A

Figure 30B

Purpose: Increase flexibility of the hamstrings, gastrocnemius, and lower back.

Starting
Position: Stride sit.

Action: Reach forward with both hands toward your ankle (see Fig. 31 A).

                Lower your head toward your right thigh. Flex the ankles to keep a constant
                stretch on the hamstrings and gastrocnemius (see Fig. 31 B).

                NOTE: Do not bounce! Reach–, hold–, reach more–, and hold. Repeat
                toward the left leg, return to starting position and repeat.

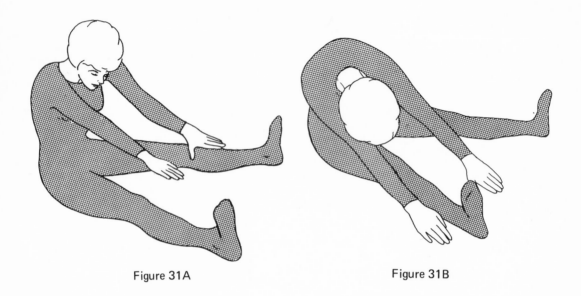

Figure 31A   Figure 31B

Purpose: Increase flexibility of the low back region.

Starting
Position: Back lying.

Action: Press the lower back firmly against the floor (see Fig. 32 A).

                Bring the knee of one leg slowly toward the chest; hold this position for
                about five counts (see Fig. 32 B).

                Slowly lower the leg to the starting position (see Fig. 32 A).

                Repeat this procedure with the other leg.

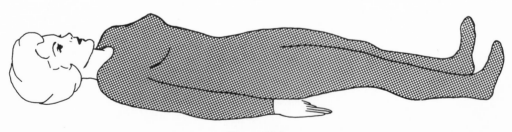

Figure 32A

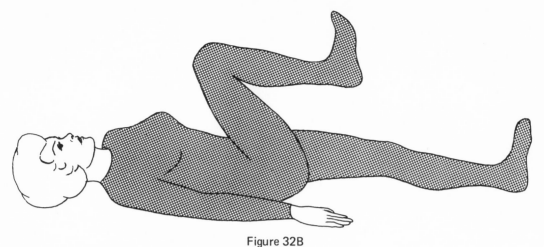

Figure 32B

Purpose:	Increase flexibility of the hamstrings.
Starting Position:	Back lying, (legs extended). Keep lower back in contact with the floor throughout the entire exercise.
Action:	Bend one knee until it is in direct line above the hip (see Fig. 33 A).

Extend leg keeping the knee straight and the ankle flexed, and hold (see Fig. 33 B).

Slowly lower the leg with the ankle still flexed to the floor. By maintaining the ankle in a flexed position, you place a stretch on the hamstring and gastrocnemius muscles in the leg.

Repeat with the opposite leg and continue until both legs have completed the exercise ten to thirty times.

Figure 33A

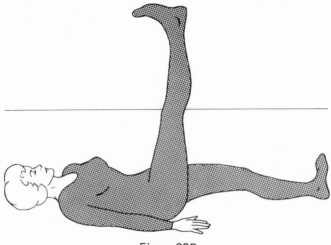

Figure 33B

Purpose: Increase flexibility of the back, neck, and hamstrings.

Starting
Position: Back lying. Place arms at a 45⁰ angle away from the sides of your body (see Fig. 34 A).

Action: Bend knees until the lower back is pressed firmly against the floor. Push downward with the palms and arms against the floor, and slowly raise the bent legs over the head (see Fig. 34 B).

As soon as your knees reach a position over your chest, fully extend both legs, flexing both ankles (see Fig. 34 C).

Continue lowering the legs until your toes touch the floor behind your head (see Fig. 34 D).

Slowly return both legs to the vertical position (see Fig. 34 C), bend the knees (see Fig. 34 B), and lower both feet to the starting position (see Fig. 34 A).

Figure 34A

Figure 34B

Figure 34C

Figure 34D

Purpose: Increase flexibility of the trunk.

Starting
Position: Tailor sit. Place both hands on your left thigh (see Fig. 35 A).

Action: Slowly turn your head to your left and at the same time press and slowly
                  pull your hands against your thigh to aid you in rotating the trunk to your
                  left, and hold (see Fig. 35 B).

                  Repeat slowly to the right and hold.

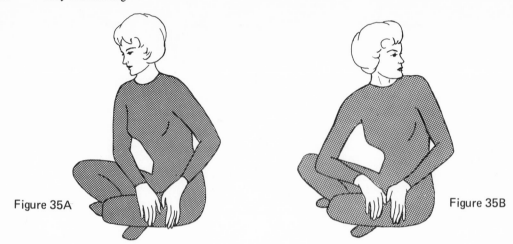

Figure 35A   Figure 35B

Purpose: Increase flexibility of the shoulder girdle.

Starting
Position: Tailor sit. Sit erect, back straight, head level and look straight ahead (see
                Fig. 36 A).

Action: Slowly lift arms from your sides, palm up, and press the arms backward
                forcing the scapula (shoulder blades) together (see Fig. 36 B).

                NOTE: Do not fling or swing the arms backward!

                Later, hold a two to five pound weight in each hand for additional resis-
                tance which will aid in strengthening the shoulder girdle.

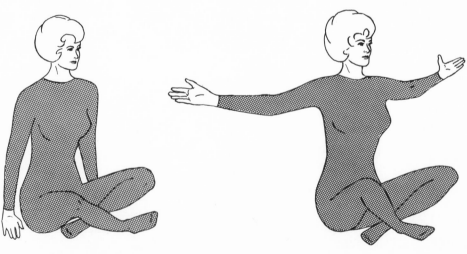

Figure 36A   Figure 36B

STRENGTH EXERCISES

Purpose: Strengthen the wrists.

Starting
Position: Sit in chair, place forearms on table with the palms of your hands facing the ceiling (see Fig. 37 A).

Action: Lift back of hands from table by bending the wrists and curling the fingers toward you (see Fig. 37 B).

For additional resistance hold a two to five pound weight in each hand while lifting back of hands from table (see Fig. 37 C).

NOTE: Keep elbow and forearm in contact with the table throughout the entire exercise.

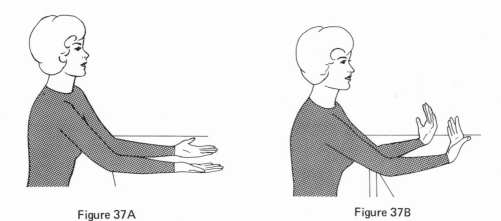

Figure 37A   Figure 37B

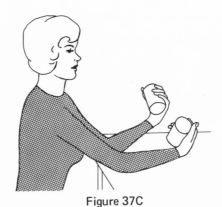

Figure 37C

Purpose: Strengthen the flexors in the fingers.

Starting
Position: Sit in chair, spread fingers apart, palm down on the table (see Fig. 38A).

Action: Firmly press the fingers downward against the table forcing the palm of the
            hand to raise from the table (see Fig. 38 B).

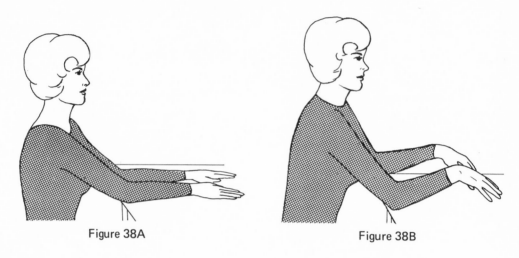

Figure 38A   Figure 38B

Purpose: Strengthen the flexors in the fingers.

Starting
Position: Sit in chair, and rest right forearm on table, allowing the hand to flop
            over the edge freely (see Fig. 39A).

Action: Enclose your hand around a small rubber ball and squeeze as hard as you
            can, relax (see Fig. 39 B).

            Repeat with the other hand.

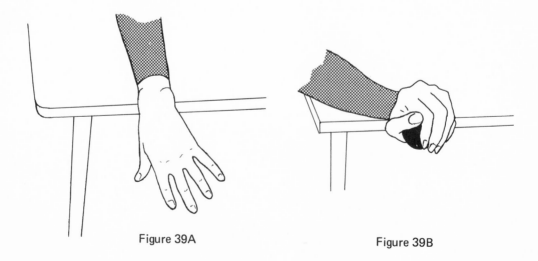

Figure 39A   Figure 39B

Purpose: Strengthen shoulder girdle and arms.

Starting
Position: Face lying. Place both hands palm down directly beneath your shoulders (see Fig. 40 A).

Action: Bend legs so that the knees and hands are the only two points in contact with the floor as you push body from the floor. Maintain body in straight line from head to knees. Keep head up and buttocks up slightly rather than down (see Fig. 40 B).

Flex elbows and lower your body until your chin touches the floor. Repeat.

NOTE: If you do not have the shoulder strength to lower the body so the chin touches the floor, then practice lowering the body about half the desired distance until you have built up sufficient strength that will allow you to perform the exercise as recommended above.

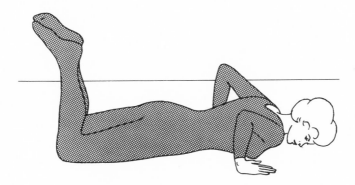

Figure 40A

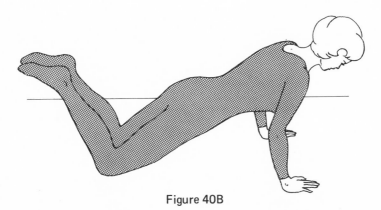

Figure 40B

Purpose: Strengthen upper arms and shoulders, stretch pectorals.

Starting
Position: Stand, spread feet shoulder-width apart in a forward and back stride position (see Fig. 41 A).

Action: Extend arms to the sides at shoulder level with palms up. Make ten small, ten medium and then ten large circles forward and then backward with both arms working together (see Fig. 41 A).

                NOTE: Do not flex elbows.

Figure 41A

Purpose   Strengthen the upper back and the abdominals.

Starting
Position: Sitting with back against a wall, knees slightly bent or legs fully extended.

Action: Press the whole spine against the wall (see Fig. 42 A).

                Place the backs of your hands and your elbows against the wall. Slowly raise the hands upward over the head, — hold (see Fig. 42 B).

                Slowly lower the arms to the floor until your finger tips touch the floor.

                NOTE: Maintain the backs of hands, elbows, and spine in a contact position with the wall throughout the entire exercise.

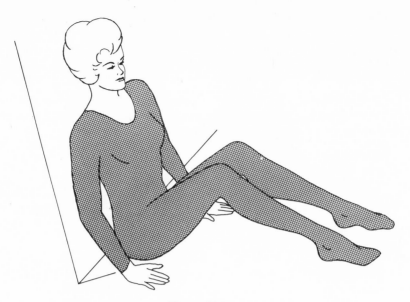

Figure 42A

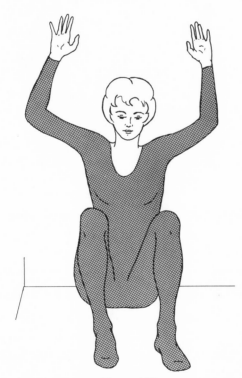

Figure 42B

Purpose: Increase abdominal strength.

Starting
Position: Back lying.

Action: Knees bent, press the lower back firmly against the floor (see Fig. 43 A).

Contraction of the abdominal and gluteal muscles will assist in pressing the lower back in a contact position with the floor.

Raise the head and shoulders from the floor with the hands placed behind your neck, and hold this position for four or five counts (see Fig. 43 B).

Slowly lower the head and shoulders to the floor (see Fig. 43 A).

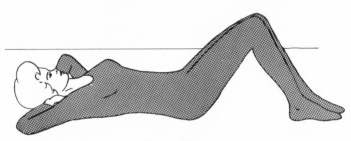

Figure 43A

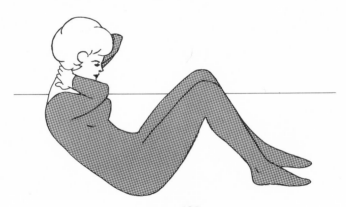

Figure 43B

Purpose: Strengthen hip extensors and quadriceps.

Starting
Position: Stand, feet slightly apart and parallel.

Action: Place hands at sides and slowly bend the trunk forward and downward (see Fig. 44 A).

Bend the right knee which is supporting your weight, at the same time raise the left leg backward and upward. Extend the arms horizontally to maintain balance and hold five to ten counts (see Fig. 44 B).

Repeat with opposite leg.

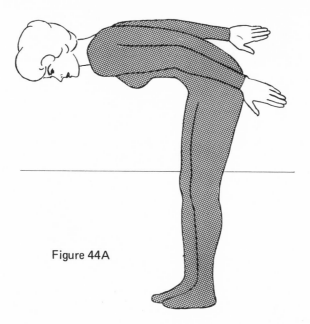

Figure 44A

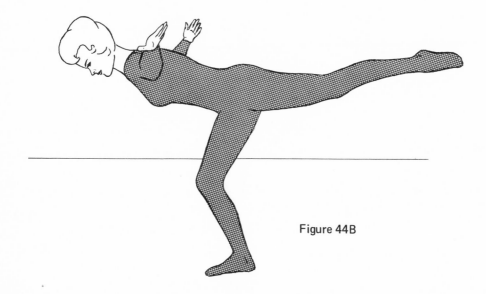

Figure 44B

Purpose: To develop strength in the quadriceps and abdominals.

Starting
Position: Kneel on floor, knees slightly apart. Support all of your weight on the knees, lower legs, and insteps of the feet (see Fig. 45 A).

Action: Slowly lean back from the knee. Trunk must remain in a straight line from your head to your knees (see Fig. 45 B).

               Slowly return to the starting position. Do not jerk your body forward quickly.

               NOTE: Contraction of the abdominal and gluteal muscles will aid you in maintaining the body in a straight line (see Fig. 45 B).

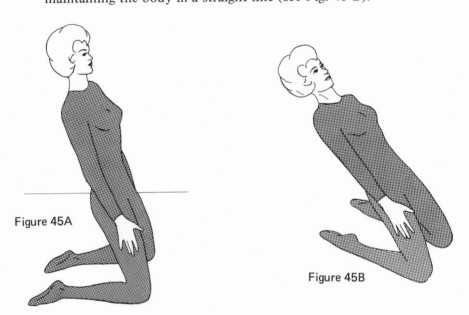

Figure 45A

Figure 45B

Purpose: Increase leg and ankle strength and endurance.

Starting
Position: Stand in place.

Action: Shift all your weight on to the right foot and hop on it ten times (see Fig. 46 A).

               NOTE: Absorb the shock of your foot striking the floor by landing on the ball of the foot throughout the entire exercise.

               Change feet and hop ten times on the left foot (see Fig. 46 B).

               Jump on both feet ten times (see Fig. 46 C).

               Hop and move the feet apart, and hop and move the feet together, repeat ten times (see Fig. 46 D).

               Alternately move the feet in a stride position ten times (see Fig. 46 E).

               Repeat entire sequence five times.

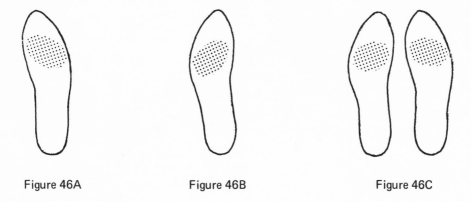

Figure 46A   Figure 46B   Figure 46C

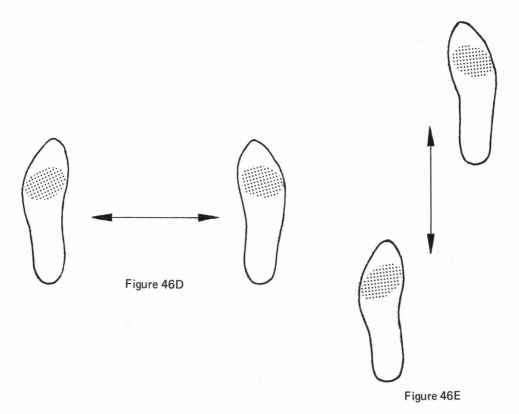

Figure 46D

Figure 46E

Purpose: Strengthen ankle extensors and arches of the feet.

Starting
Position: Stand, feet slightly apart, toes parallel (see Fig. 47 A).

Action: Slowly raise on both toes, hold four to six counts (see Fig. 47 B).

Return to starting position (see Fig. 47 A) and repeat.

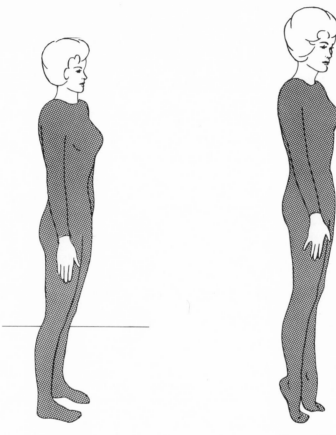

Figure 47A   Figure 47B

ROLLS AND FALLS

Some of the defensive techniques which you will practice involve one or both of the participants falling to the mat. Learn how to roll and fall properly to avoid injury. As part of your daily warm-up activity, practice one roll and one fall that you feel you will be able to master. Practice rolls and falls on mats or soft sand.

Forward Roll

Assume a squat position with weight over toes and knees together. Place your hands about shoulder distance apart, just ahead of your toes on the mat (see Fig. 48 A).

Press your chin down on to the chest as you lower your head toward your knees, keep the back rounded (see Fig. 48 B).

With both hands and feet push hard and with equal strength to insure a straight roll. As your hips come over your head, bend the elbows to ease the weight onto your shoulders and rounded back (see Fig. 48 C).

NOTE: If any part of your head touches the mat, it is because you are allowing the elbows to collapse forcing all of your weight on your head. If your back hits the mat with a jolt, it is because you are locking your elbows.

Analyze Fig. 48 C carefully. Continue roll until both feet touch the mat to place your body in the beginning squat position (see Fig. 48 D).

Reaching forward and upward with both arms out-stretched will help you maintain your balance and rise to a standing position (see Fig. 48 E).

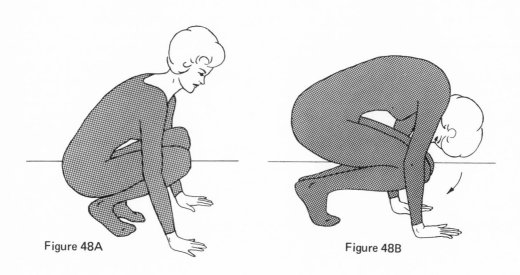

Figure 48A

Figure 48B

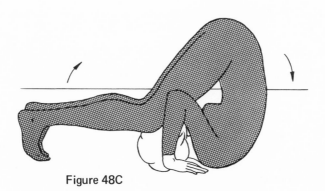

Figure 48C

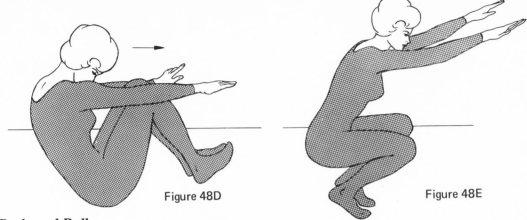

Figure 48D

Figure 48E

Backward Roll

Bend the knees and drop down on the buttocks, keeping the knees flexed and feet flat on the mat. Absorb the shock of your fall by slapping your hands on the mat at the same time that the buttocks touch the mat (see Fig. 49 A).

Place your hands at your shoulders, palms up and thumbs next to your neck. Pressing your chin against your chest, push your feet from the mat and roll backward on to your rounded back (see Fig. 49 B).

The swinging of your feet up and over your head will bring your hips vertically above your shoulders, and it is at this point that you must push hard against the mat with your hands (see Fig. 49 C).

Lower the toes down to the mat directly behind your head (see Fig. 49 D).

Continue pushing forcefully against the mat with your hands. Bend your knees as your weight shifts to the balls of the feet so that you are in a squat position (see Fig. 49 E).

Finish in a standing position ready for action (see Fig. 49 F).

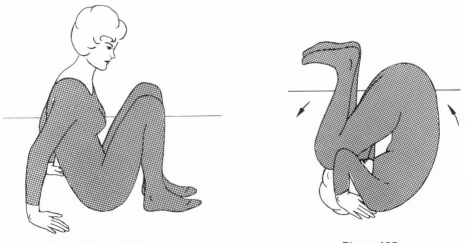

Figure 49A

Figure 49B

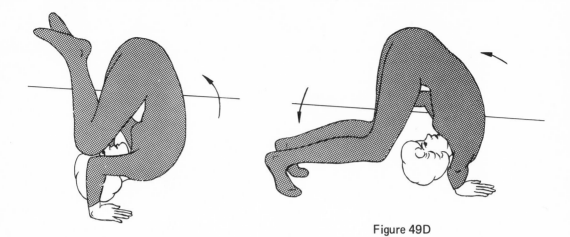

Figure 49C

Figure 49D

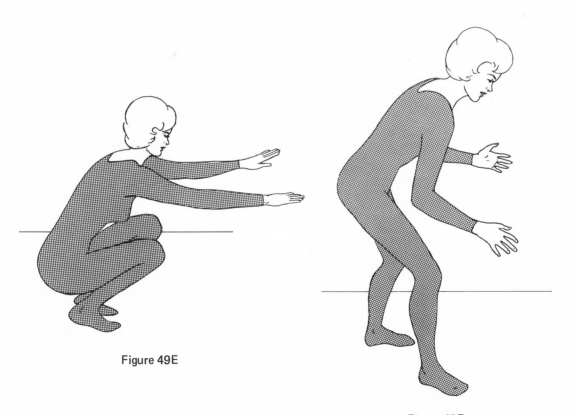

Figure 49E

Figure 49F

Shoulder Roll

Crouch down in a squat position, reach your left hand outward until it touches the mat. Place your right forearm with palm up on the mat (see Fig. 50 A).

Tuck your chin down on the chest. Push both of your feet firmly against the mat and roll forward onto your right upper back and continue rolling onto your left upper back (see Fig. 50 B).

Only your left hip and leg come in contact with the mat as you come out of the roll. Thrust your right leg forward, and at the same time reach with your hands (see Fig. 50 C).

As your left hip leaves the mat, continue rolling until your left knee and lower leg are in contact with the mat as well as your right foot (see Fig. 50 D).

From this position you can easily come to a standing position ready for action (see Fig. 50 E).

NOTE: Once this skill has been mastered from a squat position, try it from a standing and then a running approach. It is a fast roll and will cause any assailant attacking you from the rear to hesitate in wonder. The shoulder roll brings you to your feet rapidly placing you in a more advantageous position to defend yourself.

Figure 50A

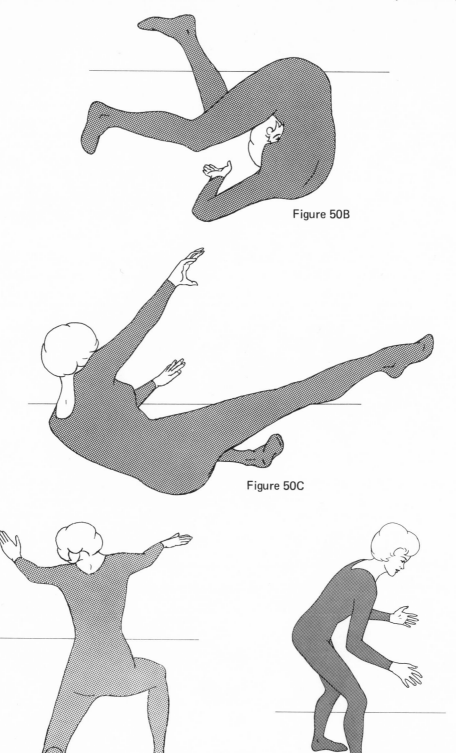

Figure 50B

Figure 50C

Figure 50D

Figure 50E

Side Fall

From a standing position flex the left knee closer and closer to the mat as you move your right foot and leg behind and across the left leg (see Fig. 51 A).

Reach directly sideward with your right arm and hand, palm down so that the fleshy part of your right hip and thigh contact the mat simultaneously with your arm and hand (see Fig. 51 B).

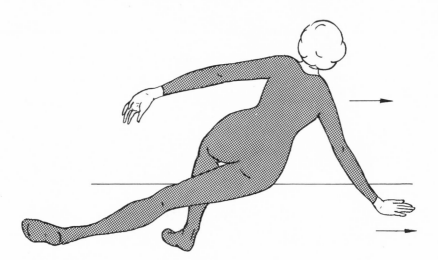

Figure 51A

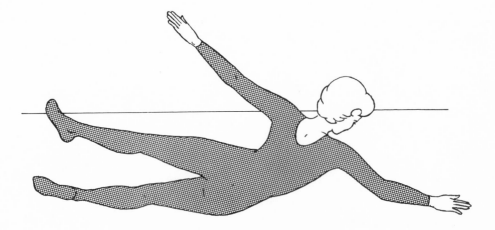

Figure 51B

Side Drop

From a standing position swing your right foot across and in front of your left foot as you flex the left knee lowering your body closer to the mat (see Fig. 52 A).

The swinging of your right foot displaces your weight so your body is suspended close to the mat in mid-air momentarily. The fleshy part of the right hip and your right hand palm down, slap the mat simultaneously to absorb the shock of your fall (see Fig. 52 B).

NOTE: Keep the hand as close to the body as possible as the hip and hand make contact with the mat. Practice the side drop on both the right and the left sides.

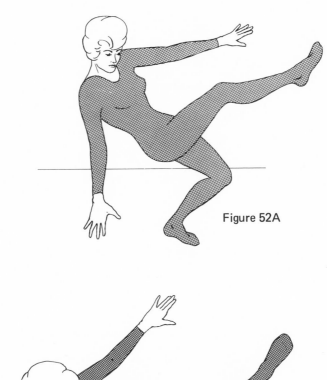

Figure 52A

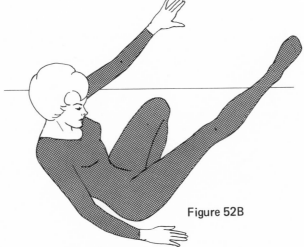

Figure 52B

Front Fall

Beginners should start in a kneeling position. Reach both arms forward and downward in a manner that will bring the palms of your hands in contact with the mat (see Fig. 53 A).

Flex both elbows simultaneously to absorb the shock of your weight as your hands strike the mat. Turn your cheek as your trunk approaches the mat (see Fig. 53 B).

In a front fall from a standing position, maintain body in a rigid position, do not flex the knees. Reach forward and downward with both hands. Fall directly forward from the ankle rather than the knees (see Fig. 53 C).

Flex the elbows as soon as the palms of your hands make contact with the mat (see Fig. 53 D).

NOTE: Turn over quickly and be ready to kick the attacker in the groin or chin with your toe. Or kick the attacker's knee, shin, pit of stomach, or solar plexus with the heel of your foot. Use both of your feet if necessary.

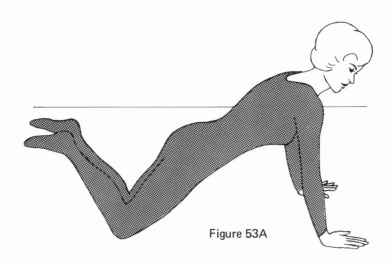

Figure 53A

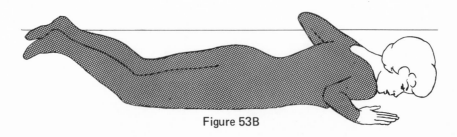

Figure 53B

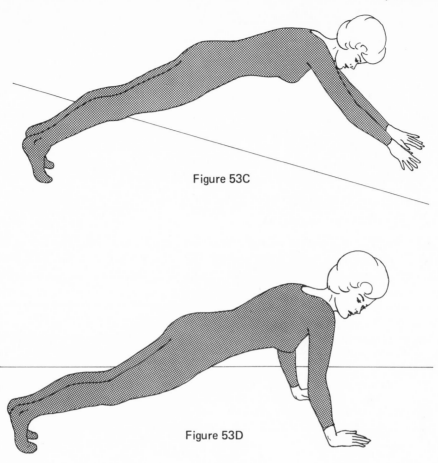

Figure 53C

Figure 53D

SUMMARY

Flexibility and strength exercises condition the body for the practice and real-life execution of personal defense techniques. An increase in range and control of motion at the joints is the desired result of the flexibility and strength exercises. In performing the body conditioning exercises, you will improve your figure as well as your fitness to meet the dangers of attack with confidence, ease, and strength.

Chapter Fourteen

PERSONAL DEFENSE TECHNIQUES

INTRODUCTION

Imagine that you are in the most dangerous situation possible; you are being strangled from the rear by an attacker. What can you do? None of the safety devices, precautions, or weapon skills learned from earlier chapters have prepared you for such a predicament. How can you, a mere woman, break the attacker's grip, incapacitate him, and escape? Personal defense techniques are the tactics of escape from an assailant's wrist grabs, body holds, strangles, and knife attacks. Regardless of your height, weight, or age — if you have done the body conditioning exercises, your body will have the flexibility and strength necessary to practice and perfect the personal defense techniques.

THE FOUR BASIC PRINCIPLES OF PERSONAL DEFENSE

All personal defense techniques are based on four principles: Balance, Focus, Advantage, and Leverage. The effectiveness of the techniques depends upon your knowledge and application of the principles to the tactics. Learn the techniques well; your life may depend on them.

1. *Balance.* Balance is the most important principle and the key to all physical maneuvers. The object of any defensive tactic is to maintain your own balance while at the same time maneuvering the attacker into a position where his balance can no longer be maintained (see Fig. 54 A, B, C, D, and E).

2. *Focus.* Apply the strength and power of your entire body at the spot of your attacker that appears to be the weakest under the circumstances. Example: Rear Body Hold. — Grab the little finger of the attacker and pull it back vigorously (see Fig. 55 A and B).

3. *Advantage.* Take advantage of the attacker's weight and momentum. A woman must assume that her attacker will be stronger than herself. Consequently, utilize your strength to direct his movements rather than to oppose him directly (see Fig. 56 A, B, C, and D).

4. *Leverage.* Use of the back and leg extensor muscles is required to gain good body leverage. Applying good body mechanics and use of proper muscle groups at the appropriate time will yield a mechanical leverage advantage regardless of your size. Skills based on the utilization of a leverage principle are throws. Example: Attacker has you in a Rear Body Hold. — Execute a hip throw by bending your knees so that your legs can do the lifting. Your hip lowered against the attacker serves as a fulcrum. From this position the attacker can be thrown easily (see Fig. 57 A and B).

DEFENSIVE TACTICS AND COUNTERS

Exercise extreme caution when learning and practicing all defensive tactics and counters. All are dangerous and can result in serious injury if practiced in a haphazard manner or without body conditioning warm-up exercises.

Practice each defensive tactic with a partner who will alternate with you in the roles of attacker and victim. The attacker should offer only passive resistance in order to aid the victim to learn the skills quickly, and to limit the possibility of injury. The victim, in executing a technique, must apply pressure slowly and must carefully simulate all striking blows. This slow motion action gives the attacker sufficient time to signal verbally, or by slapping the floor with his hand, to indicate that he is being hurt. When the attacker signals, the victim must stop applying pressure immediately before injury occurs.

All techniques practiced must stay reasonably within the limits of each person's physical capabilities. This can be done by dividing each technique into two separate phases. The first phase of any technique involves maneuvering the attacker into a position where he can be hurt by applying pressure or by being thrown. The second phase constitutes the actual throwing or application of pressure to inflict pain on the attacker. The first phase of any technique is the more important part to accomplish because it is more difficult to maneuver the attacker into a desired vulnerable position. Once you have mastered Phase I, it is an easy matter to apply pressure that will inflict pain or throw the attacker — Phase II.

The following defensive skills can be mastered by practicing Phase I and Phase II of all tactics separately. Never attempt in a real situation a technique or maneuver that you have not thoroughly mastered in practice. (Refer to Chapter 4, pp. 36-38, for a discussion on the legal rights of self-defense.)

Balance

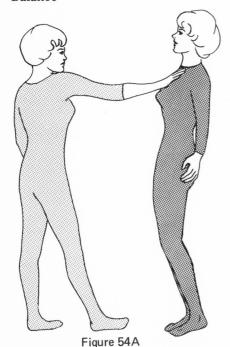

Standing with feet together, you are being pushed from the front, back, or either side. This position allows you to be pushed off balance with ease in any direction because your base of support is so small.

Figure 54A

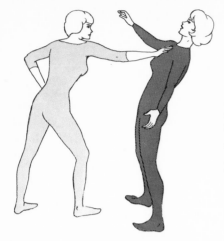

Figure 54B

Standing with the feet spread apart and your toes parallel, you are being pushed from the front or the back. You have a wider base of support; however, you would be unable to maintain your balance if pushed from the front or the back.

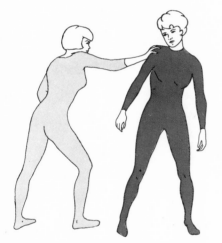

Figure 54C

Standing with the feet spread apart and your toes parallel, you are being pushed from right to left. Balance can be maintained with the feet spread apart and toes parallel only if you are being pushed directly from right to left, or vice versa.

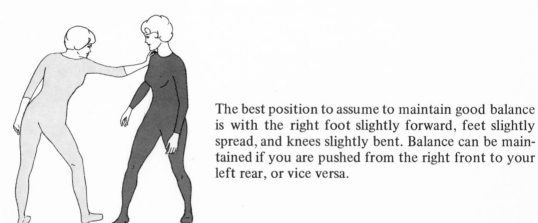

Figure 54D

The best position to assume to maintain good balance is with the right foot slightly forward, feet slightly spread, and knees slightly bent. Balance can be maintained if you are pushed from the right front to your left rear, or vice versa.

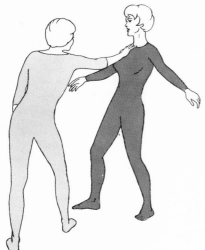

NOTE: Even in the recommended good balance position you are vulnerable if pushed from your left front to your right rear, and vice versa. To counter a push from your left front to your right rear, merely change your forward foot from right to left.

Figure 54E

Focus

The attacker has you in a rear body hold.

Phase I. Your best means of escape is to concentrate all the power and engery of your entire body against his little finger, which is the weakest part of his grasp. Use both of your hands to pry the attacker's little finger into a position where you can grasp it firmly.

Phase II. The little finger can be dislocated or broken by pulling it back forcefully.

Figure 55A

The attacker has you in a front body hold, both of your arms are free.

Phase I. Applying force to the attacker's weakest spot is again the most appropriate means of escape. Bend your knees as you place your right foot between the attacker's feet, hold your wrist firm, and spread your fingers.

Phase II. Extend your knees as you jab your fingers into the attacker's eyes. Follow-up with a right knee lift to the attacker's groin.

Figure 55B

Advantage

You attempt a haphazard defense against an attacker which agitates him, and he attempts to take you to the ground by means of a left leg tackle.

Phase I. As the attacker makes a lunge for your left leg, place one or both of your hands on his lowered head or upper back as you shift all of your weight to your right foot.

Phase II. With your hands on the attacker's lowered head or back, push down vigorously, guiding his weight and momentum toward your left. Quickly pivot on your right foot, removing your left leg from the path of the attacker to place you in a position to get away.

NOTE: When practicing Phase II of this skill, be sure the attacker is familiar with the forward roll or the shoulder roll. As the victim pushes downward on the head or upper back, the attacker should quickly tuck his chin downward against his chest and immediately roll forward.

Figure 56A

Attacker has you in a front body hold; both of your arms are free as he forces you to move backward.

Figure 56B

Phase I. Grab his clothing below the collar or upper arms. Take advantage and gain control of the backward movement by pulling the attacker forward as you suddenly sit down.

Figure 56C

Phase I. (continued). As you sit down, continue pulling the attacker forward and place your right or left foot in his mid-section or groin.

Figure 56D

Phase II. Forcefully extend the same leg, throwing the attacker over your head.

NOTE: The prime factor in bringing about the actual technique of throwing your attacker depends upon your ability to take advantage and properly direct his momentum. Practice this skill in slow motion and allow the attacker to execute a forward roll by having him reach for the floor directly behind your head. The attacker can seriously injure his back if he lands flat on his back, which is indicated in (Fig. 56 D).

PRACTICE PREPARATION:

Phase I. Sit down, grab the attacker's clothing below the collar or upper arms, place your foot in position. Let the attacker assist you.

PRACTICE PREPARATION:

Phase II. As you pull the attacker and begin extending your leg to throw him over your head, the attacker must give slight impetus by pushing off from the floor with his feet. If the attacker fails to push off with his feet, your knee will be pushed toward your chest, and you will be unable to lift the total weight of the attacker when your knee is flexed to this extent.

NOTE: If you were executing this skill in a real situation, the attacker's weight and momentum would be moving forward duplicating the slow motion practice of Phase II where the attacker aids you by pushing off from the floor.

Leverage

The attacker has you in a front body hold. (You slip your right hand and arm around his back; then, as you turn toward your left, bend forward placing your buttocks against his mid-section).

Figure 57A

Phase I. Bend your trunk forward placing your hip against the attacker's mid-section, so that your hip will serve as a fulcrum.

Figure 57B

Phase II. Throw the attacker by pulling the upper part of his body forward, simultaneously twisting your trunk vigorously to the left and extending your knees.

NOTE: Be sure the attacker is familiar with the side drop (see Fig. 52 A and B) before practicing Phase II of this skill.

WRIST AND ARM GRABS

Attacker grabs your right wrist with his left hand in a manner that places his left thumb on top and his fingers under your wrist.

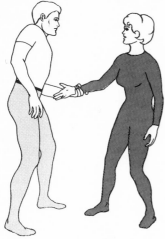

Figure 58A

Phase I. Pull the attacker toward you, or step forward with your right foot in order to get your right arm closer to your body.

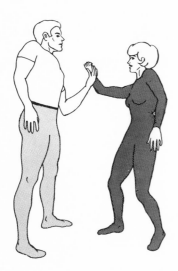

Phase II.   Forcefully twist against the attacker's thumb by lifting your arm and twisting it to your right. To gain additional power in breaking the attacker's grasp, keep your elbow close to your body as you lift and twist your arm to your right.

Figure 58B

Using both hands the attacker grasps your left wrist in a manner that places both his thumbs on top of your wrist.

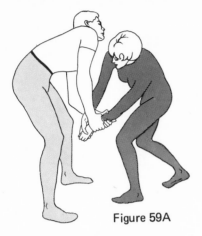

Figure 59A

Phase I. Strike an edge-of-the-hand blow (see Fig. 70C) to the side of the attacker's neck, or feint a blow to his face with your right hand.

Phase II. Step forward with your left foot, bend both of your knees, and bring your right arm closer to your body. Immediately reach your right hand between the attacker's arms and grasp your own left fist.

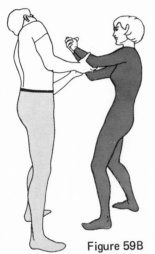

Figure 59B

Phase II (continued). Forcefully pull upward and backward as you extend your knees.

NOTE: Attacking the weakest point of the attacker's grip occurs when you apply pressure against his thumbs forcing him to release his grip.

Figure 59C

Phase II (continued). Once the attacker's grasp is released, follow up with an elbow to his chin or face.

The attacker using his right hand grabs your left upper arm just above the elbow (see Fig. 60A).

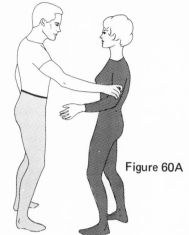

Figure 60A

Figure 60B

Phase I.   Swing your left arm toward your left, bending your elbow as your hand crosses over his right wrist. This action traps his right wrist in the crook of your left elbow.

Phase II.   Grasp the attacker's right hand with your right hand, pushing his hand backward to exert additional pressure on his wrist. Or grasp the back of your own left hand with your right hand to help exert pressure on the back of the attacker's wrist. While gripping, bend your trunk forward and pull both of your arms toward your body. Upon releasing your right hand, follow up with a blow to the attacker's face or the side of his neck.

NOTE: Be cautious when practicing Phase II because quick forceful pressure can break the wrist.

BODY HOLDS

Front Body Holds

The attacker grabs you around the body from the front; one or both of your arms are free.

Figure 61

Phase I.   Immediately bend your knees so you will be in a position of reasonably good balance.

Phase II.   Quickly follow up with a heel of the hand blow to the attacker's nose.

Attacker throws both his arms around your neck and upper back in an effort to pull your face against his chest.

Figure 62

Phase I. Quickly take one step backward with your left foot and bend both knees.

Phase II. Vigorously thrust both your fists into the attacker's groin to free yourself from his grasp.

Attacker wraps both his arms around your neck.

Figure 63A

Phase I. With your left hand grasp the attacker's clothing near his right shoulder and wrap your right arm around his body. Simultaneously and swiftly, with your right foot step across and in front of the attacker's body. Keep both knees bent and place your buttocks low against the attacker. Aid the turn about of your feet and body by pulling downward with your left hand and upward with your right arm and shoulder.

Phase II. Vigorously pull the upper part of the attacker's body forward, twist your trunk to your left, and forcefully extend your knees to throw the attacker over your right hip to the floor. Release your hand grip from the attacker just before he hits the floor, turn to your left and escape.

PRACTICE PREPARATION:

Review in slow motion all of Fig. 63A. Slowly twist your trunk toward your left as you start to extend your knees. It is at this point that the attacker's feet lose contact with the floor.

Figure 63B

As you extend your knees fully, do not pull the attacker forward with too much vigor, and continue holding on to him so he can land safely on his feet in a semi-squat position in front of you. Before practicing Phase II, Fig. 63B, be certain the attacker knows how to do the side drop (see Fig. 52A and B) on both the right and the left sides with proper hand slap.

Rear Body Holds

Attacker grasps you around the body from the rear with both of his arms; one or both of your arms are free.

Phase I. Step forward with your left foot and turn your body to the right. Raise your right arm with the elbow flexed.

Phase II. Strike and elbow blow to his face.

Figure 64

Attacker grasps you around the body from the rear with both of his arms; both of your arms are pinned to your sides (see Fig. 65A).

Figure 65A

Phase I. Bend over from your waist, shift all of your weight to your forward right foot as you twist your body to your right, place your left foot around and behind the attacker's right foot.

Figure 65B

Figure 65C

Phase II.   Immediately move your right foot back slightly to the right side of the attacker as you put your left foot between the attacker's feet, placing your hip directly behind his right buttocks. Forcefully fling both of your arms backward striking your left arm against the attacker's chest, breaking his grasp. As the attacker starts to lean backward, continue pressing your left arm against his chest and force him to drop to the floor over your left hip.

NOTE: Should the flinging of your arms backward not be sufficient to force the attacker backward, (1) shift all of your weight to your right foot and lift the attacker's right leg with your left hip and thigh as you extend your right knee, or (2) shift all of your body weight to your right foot, quickly place the ball of your left foot behind the attacker's right knee, and push his knee forward as you continue pressing your left arm against his chest. Choose one of the techniques described in Fig. 65C that works best for your size and strength, and practice the skill until you are able to execute it with ease.

Attacker steps behind you placing his right foot between your feet and wraps his arms around your neck so that both of your arms are free.

Figure 66A

Phase I.   Fake a head grasp by swinging your arms upward, then suddenly bend forward and grasp the attacker's leg near his ankle as you push your buttocks forcefully backward into the attacker's mid-section.

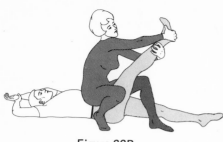

Figure 66B

Phase II. Continue pulling the attacker's leg upward as you fall backward sitting down hard on the attacker's mid-section.

NOTE: From this position you can execute a counter joint movement on his knee by pressing your knee and lower leg against his knee and thigh and pulling his leg back sharply. Get away from your attacker as soon as possible; a counter joint movement on his knee may not be necessary.

Attacker approaches you from the rear and throws his arms around your body pinning both of your arms to your sides.

Figure 67

Phase I. Move slightly toward your left until the attacker's left foot is slightly behind your feet. Keep your knees bent and lean your trunk forward from the waist.

Phase II. Immediately double your right fist and strike an edge-of-the-fist blow to his groin which will loosen the attacker's hold.

Attacker approaches you from the rear and throws both of his arms around your chest.

Figure 68A

Phase I. Swiftly shift all of your weight to your right foot as you step slightly to your right with your right foot. Swiftly move your left leg and foot behind the attacker's right foot as you bend forward from the waist. Holding your hands on the attacker's legs just above the knee will help you maintain your balance while maneuvering into this position.

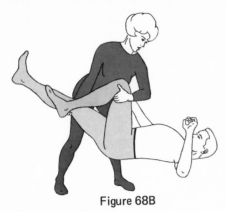

Figure 68B

Phase II.   Continue holding your hands on the attacker's legs just above his knees. Turn your head sharply to your right as you lift the attacker's feet from the floor forcing him backward. The lifting of the attacker's legs will release his hold, forcing his head and upper back to strike the floor. However, if the attacker fails to release his hold, fall sideways and to your left, landing on top of him. Keep your upper left arm and shoulder in contact with the attacker's mid-section and lower chest so that the force of your landing sideways on top of him will momentarily knock the wind out of his lungs.

STRANGLES

Front Strangles

Attacker grasps your throat with his right hand.

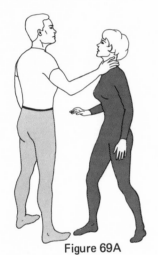

Figure 69A

Phase I.   Immediately place your right foot forward as you bend both knees.

Figure 69B

Phase II.   Sharply twist your body left as you strike his right wrist with the heel of your right hand.

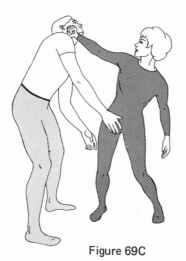

Figure 69C

Phase II (continued). Follow up with an edge-of-the-fist blow to the right side of the attacker's neck or face. An elbow blow to the face could be used effectively if the attacker is close.

NOTE: When practicing Fig. 69 B and C, go through the movements slowly and simulate your blows.

Attacker grasps your throat with both hands.

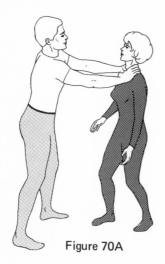

Figure 70A

Phase I. Immediately place your right foot forward as you bend both knees.

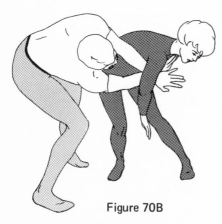

Figure 70B

Phase II. Swing your right arm upward and toward your left. Strike your upper arm and shoulder against the outside of the attacker's left wrist, stepping forward toward your left with your right foot.

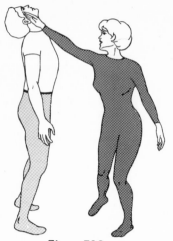

Figure 70C

Phase II (continued). Follow up with an edge-of-the-hand blow to the right side of the attacker's neck with your right hand.

Attacker grasps your throat with both his hands.

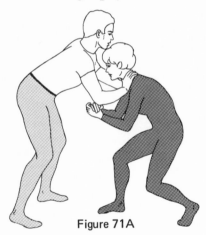

Figure 71A

Phase I.   Immediately step forward with your right foot toward the attacker. Clasp your hands together and lower your body weight by bending your knees.

Figure 71B

Phase II.   Extend your knees and forcefully bring your arms upward striking the inside of the attacker's lower arms, breaking his grasp on your throat.

Figure 71C

Phase II (continued).   Keeping your hands in a clasped position follow up with a hand blow to the attacker's face.

Rear Strangle

Attacker places his right forearm across your throat.

Figure 72A

Phase I. Grasp the attacker's right wrist with your left hand and immediately turn your head slightly to your right so you can grab a big bite of air. Bend your knees and pull down on his right forearm using your left hand. Using your right hand grasp his right arm as close to the shoulder as possible and pull him forward so that your buttocks are firmly against his mid-section.

Figure 72B

Phase II. Throw the attacker over your right shoulder by simultaneously bending your trunk forward, twisting your trunk vigorously to your left, pulling forward with both of your arms, and straightening both of your legs.

Front Strangle With The Victim Lying On Her Back On The Floor

Attacker attempts to strangle you while he is sitting on top of your mid-section.

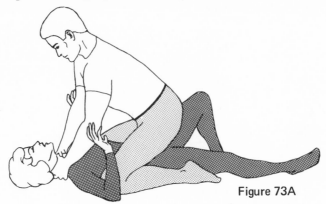

Figure 73A

Phase I. Draw your left knee toward the back of the attacker until the sole of your foot is flat against the floor. Get ready to place your thumbs on the inside of crook on the attacker's arms.

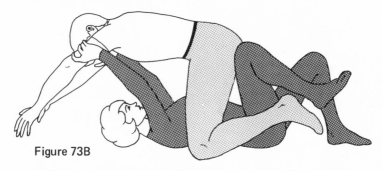

Figure 73B

Phase II. Dig your thumbs into the crook of the attacker's arms as you forcefully bring your right knee into his crotch.

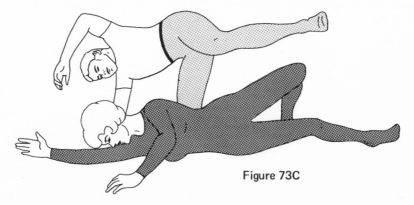

Figure 73C

Phase II (continued). Continue pushing the attacker forward and to your left forcing him off balance; swiftly roll to your right and out of the way.

Attacker is kneeling at your left side and attempts to strangle you with both of his hands.

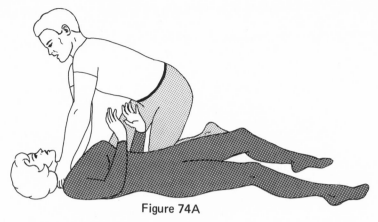

Figure 74A

Phase I. Slightly bend your knees to help you gain some leverage.

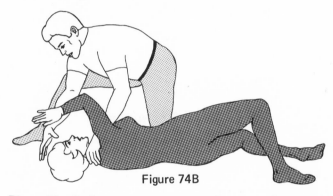

Figure 74B

Phase II. Swing your arm upward as you vigorously twist your body to your left, striking the attacker's right wrist with the heel of your right hand.

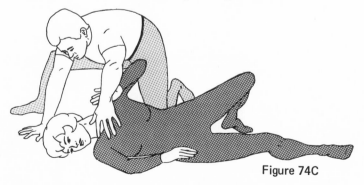

Figure 74C

Phase II (continued). Twist your body vigorously to your right and strike the attacker's left wrist with the heel of your left hand and continue rolling toward your right.

ARM LOCKS

Attacker has your left arm in an arm lock position.

Figure 75A

Phase I. Lean forward from the waist bending your knees to help relieve the pressure. Keep the right foot slightly forward as you swing your right arm backward toward the attacker's right arm and wrist.

Figure 75B

Phase II. Swiftly grab the attacker's right wrist with your right hand and pull him forward vigorously.

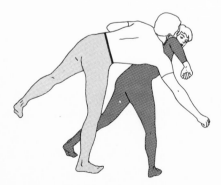

Figure 75C

Phase II (continued). Immediately twist your body to your left, and should the attacker catch his balance, flex your right elbow and strike it firmly against his ear or the side of his face.

Victim holds the attacker in a hammerlock position.

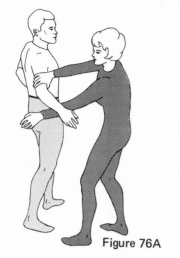

Figure 76A

Phase I.   Victim grabs the attacker's right arm just above his elbow with her right hand. The victim steps forward with her left foot as she slips her left arm under the attacker's right arm.

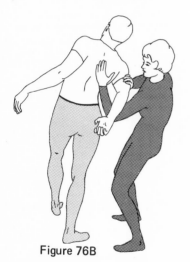

Figure 76B

Phase I (continued).   Pull the attacker's upper arm down and toward you as you bend your left elbow, placing your left hand on the attacker's upper arm just above his elbow. This position traps the attacker's wrist in the crook of your elbow.

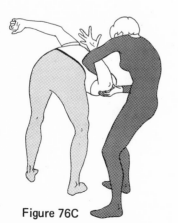

Figure 76C

Phase II.   Apply pressure to the shoulder and elbow joint by lifting your left arm upward and pushing his upper arm downward. Keep the attacker's elbow as close to your body as possible.

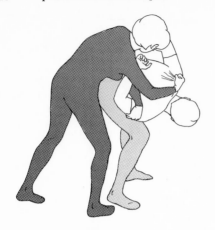

Figure 76D

Phase II (continued). If you wish to hold the attacker in this position, or if you want to lead him, be sure you grasp his left shoulder or grab a big hunk of his hair with your right hand in order to prevent the attacker from executing a counterattack.

Figure 76E

Phase II (continued). By applying sufficient pressure, the attacker's arm can be broken or his shoulder dislocated. The pain can drive the attacker to a kneeling position with his head down on the floor. You could hold him until help comes by keeping your left knee pressed against the back of his right knee.

KNIFE ATTACKS

Attacker attempts to knife you with a downward thrust.

Figure 77A

Phase I. Immediately block the attacker's wrist by forming a V with your hands. (The V is formed by placing your right thumb on your left index finger and your left thumb under your right index finger). After blocking the attacker's downward knife thrust, grasp his wrist with both of your hands forcing his hand backward.

Figure 77B

Phase I (continued). Quickly release your right hand and pass it under the attacker's arm and grasp his right wrist.

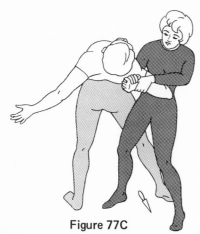

Figure 77C

Phase II. Bend the attacker backward, applying additional pressure to his wrist by pushing downward on his wrist with both of your hands and pulling upward on his arm with your right forearm causing him to drop the knife. Continue applying pressure as you place your right foot behind and inside the attacker's right foot. From this position the attacker can be thrown to the floor over your right thigh quite easily.

Attacker attempts to knife you with a downward thrust. (Use same maneuvers described in Fig. 77A).

Figure 78A

Phase I. With your left foot step toward your right, turning your back to him as you turn his arm clockwise.

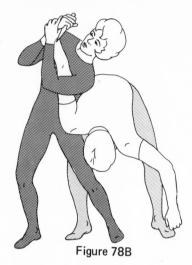

Figure 78B

Phase II. Continue to pull the attacker forward so that his elbow will be directly in front of your arm pit. The attacker will be forced to drop the knife, and his elbow will be severely injured if you lean backward and downward on his elbow as you pull his hand upward.

Attacker attempts to knife you with an upward thrust.

Figure 79A

Phase I. Block his thrust by stepping forward on your left foot, forming a V with your hands and gripping his wrist firmly.

Figure 79B

Phase I (continued). Maintain a tight grip on the attacker's wrist as you sweep his arm across and upward to your right. Simultaneously turn your body by pivoting on your right foot as you step toward your right with your left foot.

Figure 79C

Phase II. By maintaining a firm grip on the attacker's wrist as you swing his arm over your head, you will automatically turn his arm clockwise forcing the palm of his hand upward. Pulling the arm forcefully downward so that the attacker's arm lies across your shoulder and his elbow lies slightly forward of your right shoulder can break his arm or dislocate his shoulder.

Attacker attempts to knife you with an upward thrust. (Execute Phase I as described in Fig. 79A and B). However, the attacker bends his elbow behind your right shoulder so that injury to his elbow is impossible (see Fig. 80A).

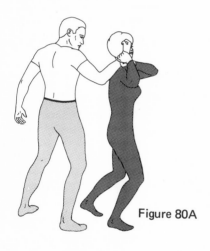

Figure 80A

Figure 80B

Phase I. Shift all of your weight to your right foot, and step across to your right with your left foot as you release your right hand. Pass your right hand under the attacker's right arm and over his wrist.

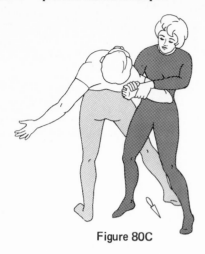

Figure 80C

Phase II. Bend the attacker backward by pushing downward on his wrist with both of your hands and pulling upward on his arm with your right forearm causing him to drop the knife.

Attacker attempts to knife you with an upward thrust.

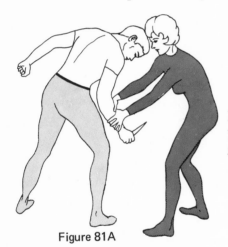

Figure 81A

Phase I. Block his thrust by stepping forward on your left foot, forming a V with your hands, and gripping his wrist firmly.

Figure 81B

Phase I (continued). Shift your weight to your left foot as you turn your body and step toward your left with your right foot. Swing the attacker's right arm over your head.

Figure 81C

Phase I (continued).   Simultaneously whip the attacker's right arm downward and push his hand up his back.

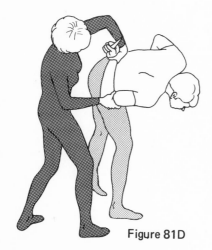

Figure 81D

Phase II. Slide your right hand toward his elbow placing the thumb of your right hand in the crook of his arm. Simultaneously thrust his wrist up his back. From this position pain can be inflicted, the arm broken, or the shoulder dislocated by pulling sharply downward on his elbow as you push his wrist upward with your left hand.

Attacker attempts to knife you with a side thrust, his palm facing upward.

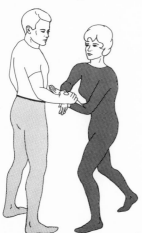

Figure 82A

Phase I. Step forward with your left foot and block the attacker's thrust by forming a V with your hands; (palms facing the attacker), immediately grasp his wrist firmly.

Figure 82B

Phase II. Step across his body and to the right with your right foot, turning his arm counterclockwise. Throw your hip hard against his mid-section as you forcefully pull his right arm upward.

NOTE: The continuous turning of the attacker's hand counterclockwise will force him to drop the knife. Applying pressure on the attacker's elbow joint by pulling his arm vigorously upward can dislocate the shoulder or break his arm.

Attacker attempts to knife you with a side thrust made from the left side of his body with his right hand.

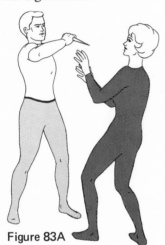

Figure 83A

Phase I. Immediately step forward with your left foot and block the thrust by forming a V with your right palm up and left palm down; grip his wrist firmly.

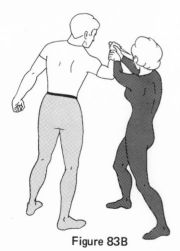

Figure 83B

Phase I (continued). Quickly step forward with your right foot directly toward the attacker as you slide the thumb of your right hand over the back of the attacker's right hand. Push the attacker's arm and hand upward and toward his right.

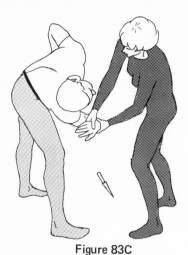

Figure 83C

Phase II. Exert pressure on the wrist by twisting his arm and wrist counterclockwise, executing a wrist throw that will force him to the floor.

SUMMARY

Direct physical contact with an attacker is the most feared threat to your personal safety; your life is in imminent danger. Counterattack and escape from such situations is the objective of personal defense techniques. The success of each defense tactic depends upon the proper application to it of the basic principles of balance, focus, advantage, and leverage. Begin each practice session with strength, flexibility, roll and fall exercises. Very carefully follow all directions.

Like all other safety and defense measures, personal defense techniques must be practiced regularly even after you have perfected them. Unused skills are like unused locks; they provide no protection. For as long as crime exists you should continue to practice safety and defense techniques in order to avoid becoming a victim of a criminal.

BIBLIOGRAPHY

Accas, Gene, and John H. Eckstein, *How To Protect Yourself On The Streets And In Your Home,* New York, Pocket Books Incorporated, 1965.

Arizona Daily Star (August 9, 1965), Section A, p. 1.

Beattie, Ronald H., *Crime In California 1964,* Sacramento, California, Bureau of Criminal Statistics, 1964.

Beattie, Ronald H., and John P. Kenney, "Aggressive Crimes," *Annals of the American Academy of Political and Social Science,* CLXIV (March, 1966), pp. 73-85.

Board of Supervisors, Los Angeles County, *Darkness On Your Door Step,* Los Angeles, Matthews Rotary Press, 1966.

Carter, Thomas, "How I'd Rob Your House," ed. by Robert J. Moskin, *Look Magazine,* XXX (May 31, 1966), pp. 28-29.

Conwell, Chic, *The Professional Thief,* ed. by Edwin H. Sutherland, Chicago, Illinois, The University of Chicago Press, 1958.

"Crime Rise: What The Record Shows," *U.S. News And World Report* (April 19, 1965), p. 6.

"Crime Runs Wild — Will It Be Halted?" *U.S. News And World Report (*August 9, 1965), pp. 64-67.

Diaz, Carmen V., *A Study Of The Ability of Eleventh Grade Girls To Apply The Principles Of Moral Law To Actual And Hypothetical Life Situations,* Fordham University, Ph.D. Dissertation, 1952.

Ennis, Philip H., *Criminal Victimization In The United States: A Report Of A National Survey,* Washington, D.C., U.S. Government Printing Office, May, 1967.

Finesilver, Sherman G., "Justice," *Vital Speeches,* XXVI (May 19, 1960), p. 669.

Hoover, J. Edgar, "An American's Challenge," *Vital Speeches,* XXIX (December 1, 1962), p. 99.

Hoover J. Edgar, *Uniform Crime Reports In The United States, 1966,* Washington D.C., U.S. Government Printing Office, 1967.

Kling, Samuel G., *Sexual Behavior And The Law,* New York, Bernard Geis Associates, 1965.

Long, Luman H., *World Almanac 1967,* New York, Newspaper Enterprise Incorporated, World Almanac Division, 1966.

Ludes, Francis J., and Harold J. Gilbert, eds., et al editorial staff, *Corpus Juris Secundum* (A Complete Restatement of the Entire American Law as Developed by All Reported Cases), Brooklyn, New York, American Law Book Company, XCIV, 1956.

McGee, Richard A., *Probation Supervision and Training,* Sacramento, California, Board of Corrections, 1964.

"Meaningless Statistics," *Time Magazine,* LXXXVIII (August 19, 1966), p. 48.

Morris, Joe Alex, "How To Lock Burglars Out," *Reader's Digest* (December, 1966), pp. 137-140.

"New Evidence Of The Terrific Spurt Of Crime In America," *U.S. News And World Report* (August 21, 1967), p. 12.

Oakes, Edwin Stacey, and George S. Gulick, eds., et al editors, *American Jurisprudence,* Rochester, New York, The Lawyers Cooperative Publishing Company, LVI, 1947.

Paradise, Jean, and Maron Loeb, et al editors, *Collier's 1967 Year Book Covering The Year 1966,* U.S.A., Crowell Collier and Macmillian Incorporated, 1967.

Penal Code Of The State Of California, Bender-Massachusetts, Bancroft-Whitney Company, 1959.

Penal Code Of The State Of California, 1966 Supplement, Bender-Massachusetts, Bancroft-Whitney Company, 1966.

Reiss, Albert J. Jr., and Albert Lewis Rhodes, "The Distribution of Juvenile Delinquency in the School Class Structure," *American Sociological Review,* XXVI (October, 1961), pp. 720-732.

"Rising Crime Is An Immediate Problem And Needs Answer Now," *The Los Angeles Times* (January 29, 1968), p. 5, col. 3-4.

Rosenberg, Bernard, Israel Gerver, and F. William Howton, *Mass Society In Crisis,* New York, The Macmillian Company, 1964.

Rosett, Arthur, "Topical Comment: Crime Crackdown, A Necessary But Expensive Project," *The Los Angeles Times* (January 21, 1968), Section G, p. 7, col. 3-5.

Schapper, Beatrice, "What We Now Know About Sex Molesters," *Today's Health* (January, 1966), pp. 18-21, 78-81.

Smith, Philip M., "Organized Religion and Criminal Behavior," *Sociology and Social Research,* XXXIII (May, 1949), pp. 362-367.

Sutherland, Edwin H., and Donald R. Cressey, *Principles of Criminology,* 7th. ed., Philadelphia, J.B. Lippincott Company, 1966.

The Los Angeles Times (June 4, 1967), Section A, p. 1.

"The Safest Large City," *American City,* LXXX (August, 1965), p. 160.

United States Senate, Committee on the Judiciary, 19th Congress 1st Session, *Controlling Crime Through More Effective Law Enforcement,* Washington, D.C., U.S. Government Printing Office, 1967.

United States Senate, Legislative Reference Service, Library of Congress, 90th Congress 1st Session, *Combating Crime In The United States,* Washington, D.C., U.S. Government Printing Office, Document XXVI, May, 1967.

Vogel, Victor H., M.D., *Facts About Drug Addiction,* Chicago, Illinois, Science Research Associates, 1965.

Weinberger, Caspar W., "New York Proposal To Loosen Police Curbs Has Merit," *The Los Angeles Times,* February 2, 1968, Part II, p. 5, col. 1-2.

Clip out order form and send to:

BURGESS PUBLISHING COMPANY
426 South Sixth Street
Minneapolis, Minnesota 55415

GIVE THIS ORDER FORM TO A FRIEND. YOU CAN HELP A FRIEND, NEIGHBOR, OR RELATIVE AVOID BECOMING A VICTIM OF A CRIMINAL.

I WISH TO ORDER THE FOLLOWING BOOKS:

Please send _____ copies of

PERSONAL SAFETY AND DEFENSE FOR WOMEN by F.P. Stock $3.75.

☐ **Please charge to my account**   ☐ **Send post-free, payment enclosed**

NAME _____

ADDRESS _____

CITY _____ **STATE** _____ **ZIP** _____

B1